PATHWAYS TO CHANGE

PATHWAYS TO CHANGE
Brief Therapy Solutions with Difficult Adolescents

Matthew D. Selekman

THE GUILFORD PRESS
New York / London

© 1993 The Guilford Press
A Division of Guilford Publications, Inc.
72 Spring Street, New York, NY 10012

Printed in the United States of America

This book is printed on acid-free paper.

Last digit is print number: 9   8   7   6   5   4   3

Library of Congress Cataloging-in-Publication Data

Selekman, Matthew, D., 1957–
    Pathways to change : brief therapy solutions with difficult
adolescents / by Matthew D. Selekman.
        p.   cm.
    Includes bibliographical references and index.
    ISBN 0-89862-015-5
    1. Brief psychotherapy for teenagers.   I. Title.
    [DNLM: 1. Psychotherapy, Brief—in adolescence. 2. Psychotherapy,
Brief—methods.   WS 463 S464p 1993]
RJ504.3.S45   1993
616.89'022—dc20
DNLM/DLC
for Library of Congress   93-848
                                                                 CIP

PREFACE

Isn't the Solution-Oriented model a band-aid approach?

What about clients' feelings, where do they fit into this model?

Can this approach really work with serious and chronic adolescent problem cases?

What do you do when the Solution-Oriented approach doesn't work?

Questions like these from colleagues, workshop participants, and trainees, have challenged me over the years to look for new ways to expand the basic Solution-Oriented Brief Therapy model and make it more integrative, particularly with adolescent cases that have been labeled "difficult," "resistant," and "bottom-of-the-barrel" therapeutic failures. The impetus for writing this book evolved out of my desire to provide answers to the above questions and offer clinicians useful therapeutic options when the basic Solution-Oriented Brief Therapy model is not working.

This book is also about therapeutic improvisation and play in brief therapy, a neglected area in the literature. It is my contention that therapy should be fun, particularly with adolescents and their families. The traditional belief that "therapy is serious business" is an unhelpful idea that has handicapped therapists. Finally, my overall hope is that this book will provide brief therapists with useful guidelines for therapeutic decision making, stimulate creative ingenuity, and offer the requisite skills for doing effective therapeutic work with challenging adolescents and their families.

Overview of the Book

This book is specifically designed to provide clinicians with the practical "how-to's" for conducting my Solution-Oriented Brief Family Therapy approach with difficult adolescents and their families. Chapter 1 describes the evolution of the Solution-Oriented Brief Therapy model, particularly its expansion to incorporate innovative ideas from the family therapy field. Chapter 2 presents helpful assumptions about difficult adolescents, their families, and brief therapy. Chapter 3 discusses how to cocreate a context for change in the very first family interview. Several different categories of therapeutic questions and guidelines for intervention design, selection, and implementation will be presented.

Chapters 4 and 5 address two important gaps in the brief therapy literature. Chapter 4 presents five effective and empirically based engagement strategies that can be utilized with difficult adolescents. Chapter 5 discusses the therapeutic effectiveness of organizing and collaborating with the difficult adolescent's social ecology of involved helping professionals and significant others. Several case examples are provided in both of these chapters.

In Chapter 6, I present a variety of strategies for amplifying changes and consolidating therapeutic gains in the second and subsequent therapy sessions. Pattern intervention, treatment team strategies, Solution-Oriented therapeutic tasks, and other therapeutic options for challenging cases are discussed.

Chapter 7 presents the Solution-Oriented parenting group. The parenting group is designed to capitalize on the strengths and resources of parents to co-construct solutions. A session-by-session description is provided. Finally, Chapter 8 summarizes the major themes of the book and offers some implications for the future.

ACKNOWLEDGMENTS

There are several important people I wish to thank for greatly contributing to my professional development and to the ideas discussed in this book. To begin with, I am indebted to Michele Weiner-Davis for showing me the short road to change. While continuing on this road, I had some important training experiences with Eve Lipchik, Steve de Shazer, and Insoo Berg that served to further develop my brief therapy skills. I would like to thank Michael White and Michael Durrant for showing me the effective therapeutic pathway of "externalizing the problem." I am indebted to the late Harry Goolishian and to Harlene Anderson for teaching me the importance of the family's story, the art of collaborating with helpers from larger systems, and the therapeutic tool of "not-knowing." More recently, I have found the innovative reflecting team approach of Tom Andersen to be most useful in my clinical work. I would like to thank the Beech Grove Children's Centre clinical team in Kingston, Ontario, for providing me with a training context in which to conceptualize and generate new therapeutic ideas. Finally, I would like to thank my friend and colleague Tom Todd for his encouragement and support over the years.

There are a number of key people that are responsible for paving the way for the creation of this book. I owe a big thanks to Sharon Panulla of The Guilford Press for providing me with this wonderful opportunity to put my clinical ideas into print. I want to thank Don Efron for his helpful editorial comments and feedback on the manuscript, and also Patricia Talamo, a highly skilled court reporter, who had the herculean task of transcribing several videotapes of the case examples presented in the book. Vivian Sena and Sandra Biles of Robinson's Office Services deserve gold medals for their patience and good cheer while they painstakingly typed this manuscript. Finally and foremost, I would like to thank Åsa, my loving wife, for her support and patience throughout this whole process.

CONTENTS

PATHWAYS TO CHANGE

O N E

AN EVOLVING BRIEF THERAPY MODEL FOR DIFFICULT ADOLESCENTS

THERAPIST: What would you like to change today?

MOTHER: Well, Jennifer is pulling her hair out again. I think our family doctor called it trichotillomania, something like that.

JENNIFER: Yeah, it's kind of like a bad habit I've had for a long time.

M: Yeah, she has been pulling out her hair on and off for the past four years.

T: I'm curious, what's happening during the times when this "bad habit" is not pushing you around, what are you doing instead?

J: Well, I'm listening to "Guns and Roses," talking to my friend Linda, or doing my homework . . .

T: How did you come up with all of those great ideas for helping you stand up to the "bad habit"!?

J: Well, "Guns and Roses" helps me relax. Linda and I like to talk about all of the cute boys at school. It seems like when I keep busy that helps a lot.

T: Jennifer, can you think of anything your mom does that helps you fight off the "bad habit"?

J: Yeah . . . some nights we talk about the boys, you know, when she was my age . . . sometimes, she lets me rent a video that we watch together that relaxes me too.

In order to protect client confidentiality, all names and client identifying background information have been changed in the case examples described within this book.

Many therapists would consider Jennifer's presenting problem alarming and quite difficult to treat. Prior to this first family session, the intake worker found out from the mother that Jennifer had been in therapy three times before for her "compulsive hair pulling" problem. One of the past therapists had been a psychiatrist who had labeled Jennifer as having obsessive compulsive disorder. Despite the chronicity of Jennifer's hair-pulling problem, I believed strongly that Jennifer and her mother had the strengths and resources to change. I capitalized on Jennifer's description of the problem as being a "bad habit" and externalized it into an oppressive symptom (White & Epston, 1990) that had been pushing both Jennifer and her mother around for some time. This opened up many more avenues for change than the doctors' labels of "obsessive compulsive disorder" and "trichotillomania." Finally, I invited Jennifer and her mother to share with me what they were doing that was preventing the "bad habit" from pushing them around. This line of questioning elicited from the family "change talk" (Gingerich, de Shazer, & Weiner-Davis, 1988), that is, effective coping and problem-solving strategies that could serve as building blocks toward co-constructing a solution.

The family wellness approach I was utilizing with Jennifer and her mother is my Solution-Oriented Brief Family Therapy approach, which is an expansion of the Solution-Oriented Brief Therapy model developed by O'Hanlon and Weiner-Davis (1989). Surprisingly, the basic Solution-Oriented Brief Therapy model has received very little attention in the brief therapy and family therapy literature as a useful model of treatment for such difficult adolescent populations as delinquents, self-mutilators, violent youth, substance abusers, and adolescents with eating disorders, school problems, and depression (Berg & Gallagher, 1991; Selekman, 1989a, 1989b, 1991b). In this chapter, I will provide a theoretical overview of the basic Solution-Oriented Brief Therapy model, describe four ways in which I have expanded the model to make it more comprehensive and effective with difficult adolescents and their families, and reflect on some common themes of difficult adolescent cases.

THEORETICAL INFLUENCES

The Solution-Oriented Brief Therapy approach was developed by William H. O'Hanlon and Michele Weiner-Davis (O'Hanlon, 1987; O'Hanlon & Weiner-Davis, 1989; Weiner-Davis, 1992). The model is heavily based on the therapeutic ideas of the brilliant hypnotist Milton H. Erickson (Erickson, 1954, 1964; Erickson & Rossi, 1983; Erickson, Rossi, & Rossi, 1976; Rosen, 1982), the Solution-Focused Brief Therapy approach developed by Steve de Shazer and his colleagues (de Shazer, 1982, 1984, 1985, 1988, 1991; de Shazer et al., 1986; Gingerich & de Shazer, 1991; Gingerich et al., 1988; Lipchik, 1988; Lipchik & de Shazer, 1986; Weiner-Davis, de Shazer, & Gingerich, 1987); and the Brief Problem-Focused Therapy approach of the Mental Research Institute (MRI) theorists (Fisch, Weakland, & Segal, 1982; Watzlawick, Weakland, & Fisch, 1974).

MILTON H. ERICKSON: THE FATHER OF BRIEF THERAPY

Erickson's contributions to the fields of hypnosis, brief therapy, and family therapy are numerous. Long after his death, his creative genius and therapeutic wizardry continue to have a major influence on therapists worldwide. Two of Erickson's most important therapeutic interventions are the utilization strategy (Erickson & Rossi, 1983; Gordon & Meyers-Anderson, 1981; O'Hanlon, 1987) and "pseudo-orientation in time" (Erickson, 1954).

Erickson believed it was essential for therapists to capitalize on whatever their clients brought to therapy: their language, beliefs, strengths and resources, sense of humor, and nonverbal behaviors. He would then utilize these client attributes in the interviewing process and with the construction of therapeutic tasks.

With the "pseudo-orientation in time" (Erickson, 1954) intervention, Erickson would first place the client in a trance and then help him or her create a sense of time distortion. This paved the way for the client to move back and forth in time. Once the client was trained in time distortion, Erickson would help the client master the skill of amnesia, then direct the client to a time in the future when he or she had successfully resolved the presenting problem. Erickson would ask the client to visualize an encounter with him in this imagined future in which the client would tell Erickson how he or she had resolved the problem. Following this step, Erickson would have the client develop amnesia for the experience and terminate therapy (O'Hanlon & Weiner-Davis, 1989).

Besides the utilization and "pseudo-orientation in time" interventions, Erickson injected an element of surprise, playfulness, and humor into his therapeutic work. Erickson once said, "Every child likes a surprise" (Rosen, 1982). He had an amazing ability to bring out the playful child in clients, capture their interest, and provoke them in the direction of change. Erickson believed that therapists should "spread humor knee deep everywhere" with clients (Rosen, 1982). He could skillfully find the humorous twists in any client's presenting problems. Erickson believed that humor had tremendous healing power. For Erickson, humor took the sting out of a painful situation and it gave clients the courage to take risks and make changes.

Erickson was a masterful storyteller. His stories incorporated humor, metaphor, embedded commands, the inclusion of interesting information, and the theme of a quest (Rosen, 1982). Erickson's stories provided a direct pipeline into the unconscious mind of the client and successfully altered outmoded beliefs and created new possibilities for the client.

In my clinical practice with adolescents, I frequently utilize metaphors and stories to indirectly influence the adolescents' unhelpful thinking and behaviors. Besides sharing my own personal struggles as a youth, I like to utilize Native American stories that offer the adolescent valuable learnings and wisdom. I once worked with a highly oppositional 16-year-old boy who refused to follow his parents' rules, do anything around the house, and basically had been on strike as a family member for 1 year. Prior to seeing me, the boy had been placed in a psychiatric hospital for 2 months and had had three unsuccessful outpatient treatment experiences with psychologists. When asked about what he wanted from his parents, the boy would say, "A black leather jacket." According to the parents, their son had been obsessing nonstop for a year about the black leather jacket they would not buy for him. After three family sessions, the parents had made some important changes, however their son was still obsessing about the black leather jacket and not responding to their rules. In the fourth family session, during my individual session time with the boy, I shared the following Native American story, as originally told by the Hoh Indian elder, Leila Fisher, on "how wisdom comes" (Wall & Arden, 1990):

> There once was a man, a postman on the reservation, who heard some of the Elders talking about receiving objects that bring great power. He didn't know much about such things, but he thought to himself that would be a wonderful thing if he could receive such an object which can only be bestowed by the Creator. In particular he heard from the Elders that the highest such object a person can receive is an eagle feather. He decided that was the one for him. If he could just receive an eagle feather he would have all of the power, wisdom, and prestige he desired. But he knew he couldn't buy one. It just had to come to him somehow by the Creator's will. Day after day he went around looking for an eagle feather. He figured one would come his way if he just kept his eyes open. It got so he thought of nothing else. The eagle feather occupied his thoughts from sunup to sundown. Weeks passed, then months, then years. Every day the postman did his rounds, always looking for that eagle feather—looking just as hard as he could. He paid no attention to

his family and friends. He just kept his mind fixed on that eagle feather. But it never seemed to come. He started to grow old, but still no feather. Finally, he came to realize that no matter how hard he looked, he was no closer to getting the feather than he had been the day he started. One day he took a break by the side of the road. He got out of his little jeep and had a talk with the Creator. He said: "I'm so tired of looking for that eagle feather. Maybe I'm not supposed to get one. I've spent all of my life thinking about that feather. I've hardly given a thought to my family and friends. All I cared about was that feather, and now life has just about passed me by. I've missed out on a lot of good things. Well, I'm giving up the search. I'm going to stop looking for that feather and start living. Maybe I have time enough to make it up to my family and friends. Forgive me for the way I have conducted my life." Then— and only then—a great peace came into him. He suddenly felt better inside than he had in all these years. Just as he finished his talk with the Creator and started getting back to his jeep, he was surprised by a shadow passing over him. He looked up into the sky and saw, high above, a great bird flying over. Almost instantly it disappeared. Then he saw something floating down ever so lightly on the breeze—a beautiful tail feather. It was his eagle feather! He realized that the feather had come not a single moment before he had stopped searching and made his peace with the Creator. That postman is now a changed person. People came to him for wisdom now and he shares everything he knows. Even though now he has the power and the prestige he searched for, he no longer cared about such things. He was concerned about others, not himself. So now you know how wisdom comes. (pp. 74–75)

After telling this wonderful Indian story to my young client, which in many ways mirrored his situation, he made a 360° turn behaviorally. One week later, the parents reported that their son had miraculously changed back into his "old self again." He was interacting with family members, following the parental rules, and doing his chores. Not once did the boy make mention of the "black leather jacket." The family and I mutually agreed to terminate therapy after a 2-week vacation break from therapy due to the identified client's tremendous progress.

SOLUTION-FOCUSED BRIEF THERAPY

The Solution-Focused Brief Therapy model was developed by de Shazer and his colleagues at the Brief Family Therapy Center in Milwaukee, Wisconsin (de Shazer, 1985, 1988, 1991; de Shazer et al., 1986; Gingerich & de Shazer, 1991; Gingerich et al., 1988; Lipchik, 1988; Lipchik & de Shazer, 1986; Weiner-Davis et al., 1987). The model is strongly influenced by the clinical work of Erickson and the theoretical ideas of Gregory Bateson. De Shazer and his colleagues built their model around the core assumption that all clients have the strengths and resources to change and the idea that no problem happens all of the time—there are exceptions to the rule. Through capitalizing on the clients' strengths and resources and having them engage in "change talk" (Gingerich et al., 1988), de Shazer and his team found that this type of therapeutic activity led to rapid changes in the clients' beliefs and behaviors. Like Erickson, de Shazer and his colleagues utilized the future to co-construct hypothetical solutions with clients. De Shazer expanded on Erickson's "pseudo-orientation in time" intervention through the use of an imaginary crystal ball (de Shazer, 1985) and eventually developed his most popular and potent therapeutic question—the "miracle question" (de Shazer, 1988). The client is asked:

> "Suppose you were to go home tonight, and while you were asleep, a miracle happened and this problem was solved. How will you know the miracle happened? What will be different?" (p. 5)

Oftentimes, the clients' reported miracles are behaviors that they can and may already be doing. The miracle question frequently generates useful exceptions and treatment outcome goals. According to de Shazer (1990), if a client can envision a future reality without problems, then they really do not have a problem.

De Shazer and his colleagues have developed several effective therapeutic tasks that are carefully matched with the unique cooperative response patterns of the clients. For example, to a vague client, de Shazer would most likely give an equally vague task like the "formula first session task" (de Shazer, 1985), which is as follows:

> "Between now and the next time we meet, I would like you to notice what is happening in your family that you would like to continue to happen." (p. 137)

In my own clinical work, I have found that approximately 90% of the time that clients have reported at least two or more important exceptions in second sessions after having been given the formula first session task.

Two other useful therapeutic tasks designed by de Shazer are the "prediction task" (de Shazer, 1988) and more recently, "pretend the miracle happened" (de Shazer, 1991). The prediction task is particularly useful when the client's exceptions occur spontaneously and they cannot account for their occurrence. For example, a depressed adolescent and her parents could be asked separately to predict the night before whether the next day will be an "up day," and in the middle of the next day, try and account for why it was an "up day." According to de Shazer (1988), "prediction tasks are based on the idea that what you expect to happen is more likely to happen once the process leading up to it is in motion" (p. 184).

The "pretend the miracle happened" task can be utilized when the clients cannot readily identify any significant exceptions (de Shazer, 1991; Gingerich & de Shazer, 1991). The following case example demonstrates the utility of this therapeutic task.

George was brought for therapy because he and his mother were constantly "arguing" and he refused to do any "chores around the house." According to George, his mom was constantly "bitching" at him. After a few of the "big arguments," George had punched holes in his bedroom wall. In an effort to move the family away from problem talk, I asked the miracle question. The mother's miracles consisted of George "emptying the garbage," "straightening up" his bedroom by putting his "dirty clothes in the laundry hamper," and no longer arguing with her. George's miracles were his mother's no longer "bitching" at him, giving him "more space time" away and more "time with friends," and cooking some of his "old favorite" dishes, for example, fried chicken. In the latter part of the session, I met alone with George and gave him the task of picking 2 days over the next week to pretend to engage in some of his mother's miracle behaviors to try and "blow her mind." He was told not to tell her which days he was pretending, but to notice how she responds differently to him. Later in the session, the mother was asked to be like a Sherlock Holmes detective and try to guess which days he was pretending. One week later, George and his mother came into the session looking like a new family. The mother's opening comments were "this is not my son." Apparently, George had been engaging in "miracle behavior all week." He had emptied the garbage and cleaned up his bedroom, and there had not been one argument all week. In fact, the mother was so pleased with George's progress that she had allowed him to "stay out later on the weekend" and had cooked "fried chicken" for him one night. I spent the entire second interview amplifying the many exceptions that had occurred and gave them a 3-week vacation from therapy as a vote of confidence. While on vacation, they were instructed to keep track of what is working in their relationship so they could come back and tell me what further progress they made. Therapy was terminated after the third session.

There are many other useful Solution-Focused therapeutic tasks that will be presented throughout the remainder of the book. In Chapter 3, I will discuss in more detail the miracle question and other therapeutic questions that can open up space for clients to view their problem situations differently, help generate exception material, and assist clients with setting realistic, well-formed treatment goals.

MRI BRIEF PROBLEM-FOCUSED THERAPY

The Brief Problem-Focused Therapy model was developed by Weakland, Jackson, Watzlawick, and Fisch at the MRI in Palo Alto, California (Fisch et al., 1982, Watzlawick, Beavin, & Jackson, 1967; Watzlawick et al., 1974). Similar to the Solution-Focused Brief Therapy group, the MRI theorists were also heavily influenced by the ideas of Erickson and Bateson. The MRI theorists built their brief therapy approach around the core assumption that it is the cient's attempted solution that is the problem (Watzlawick et al., 1974). Family members are "stuck" viewing the identified client in one particular way and engaging in the same problem-maintaining interactive dance. For the MRI theorists, the main targets for intervention are the family's belief system or "position" (Fisch et al., 1982) about the problem and the problem-maintaining patterns.

The MRI theorists have developed several therapeutic tasks that are quite useful with difficult adolescent cases. One MRI last-resort intervention that I have had success with is "benevolent sabotage" (Watzlawick et al., 1974). This task is particularly useful for highly rebellious, acting-out adolescents who are running the household and do not respond well to the Solution-Oriented Brief Therapy approach. In these cases, the more the parents try to exert their power and authority over their adolescent, the more the latter rebels. The parents are instructed to pretend that they are weak and not "themselves these days" around their adolescent. For example, the mother may pour salt rather than sugar in the cake batter when baking her son's favorite cake. The parents may lock up the house at night and accidentally leave the chains on the doors. When confronted by their adolescent, they simply say "I'm not myself these days." The adolescent will soon learn that it is impossible to rebel against weak parents (Watzlawick et al., 1974). The following case example illustrates the utility of this therapeutic strategy with a difficult 15-year-old girl and her mother.

Louise, a single parent, brought Mandy to my clinic for therapy following Mandy's discharge from a psychiatric adolescent in-patient program. Mandy had been in the hospital for 6 weeks due to her running away, school truancy, violation of parental rules, and poly-drug-abuse problems. Prior to her hospitalization, Mandy and her mother had had seven unsuccessful therapy experiences for the same presenting problems. Although Mandy came to the first family session, she spoke very little in the interview. Louise spent the majority of the session time talking about problems and all of her unsuccessful attempted solutions. My efforts to have her and Mandy identify exceptions went nowhere. Neither family member could envision future miracle changes in each other's behaviors. When I matched their pessimistic stance and inquired about how they had prevented things from getting worse, mother responded, "Sooner or later something terrible will happen to Mandy." I spent individual session time with both Mandy and her mother. Louise agreed to experiment with an observation task (Molnar & de Shazer, 1987) to help us identify some exception patterns and do something different around Mandy. Mandy made it clear to me that she "hated counselors" and would "not be back" to see me again. Sessions 2 through 4 were with Louise alone. Mandy had refused to come to anymore sessions. By this time, Louise was feeling totally frustrated and ready to throw in the towel with therapy. I decided to abandon my basic Solution-Oriented Brief Therapy approach and offer Louise, as a last-ditch attempt, the benevolent sabotage task (Watzlawick et al., 1974). Surprisingly, Louise was ready and willing to try out one more therapeutic task.

During the following week, Louise put on an Academy Award performance as a "depressed mother ready to give up her role as a mother." In fact, her performance was so successful that Mandy's behaviors dramatically changed. According to Louise, Mandy remained "drug-free," she was "attending school" again, she was "following" the "rules," and Mandy had "agreed to come back to therapy." In our fifth family session, Mandy appeared to be both confused and concerned by her mother's behavior. I shared with Mandy my concerns about her mother and explored with her what she thought she needed to continue to do to try and "lift" her mother's "spirits." Mandy suggested that she would have to "stop partying," "go to school," and "help Mom out around the house." I asked Mandy if she thought this would be enough and she agreed to "come up with some more things" that would make her mother "happy." In my individual session time with Louise, I encouraged her to do more of what was working. Future sessions involved consolidating the family's gains and collaborating with school personnel.

Other useful strategies developed by the MRI theorists are: paradoxical prescriptions, reframing, restraint from immediate change, positioning, and prediction. In *The Tactics of Change,* Fisch and his colleagues (1982) offer some very practical ideas regarding useful ways to maintain therapeutic maneuverability with some of the most difficult clients. These ideas have been particularly useful to me in my work with court-ordered youth and their families.

EXPANSION OF THE SOLUTION-ORIENTED MODEL

As do all therapy models, the basic Solution-Oriented Brief Therapy approach (O'Hanlon & Weiner-Davis, 1989) has its limitations with some highly entrenched and traumatized families, as well as with chronic adolescent cases that are riddled with multiple helpers from larger systems. Therefore, to incorporate more therapeutic flexibility and make the basic Solution-Oriented Brief Therapy approach more comprehensive, I have integrated innovative ideas from renowned jazz improvisors (such as Charlie Parker), and from the therapeutic approaches of Michael White, the Galveston team (Harry Goolishian and Harlene Anderson) and Tom Andersen. I will begin this section of the chapter by discussing how the use of improvisational techniques can help therapists enjoy their work more and strengthen their creative capacities. This will be followed by a brief discussion of some of the major therapeutic strategies of Michael White, the Galveston team, and Tom Andersen that I like to utilize when working with difficult adolescents and their families. Finally, I will conclude this section by discussing the importance of brief therapists' collaboration with involved helpers from larger systems.

BRIEF THERAPIST AS AN IMPROVISATIONAL ARTIST

Anything and everything goes in my therapy sessions—there are no rules! From "high fives" to outrageous humor, I strive to create a therapeutic climate that is playful and full of surprises. Each new adolescent case is approached with passion, spontaneity, and playful use of humorous elements of the family's story. Besides the use of humor and play, therapeutic improvisation can also take the form of telling stories, doing something dramatic in the therapy session, and testing out a therapeutic strategy from a different therapy approach. For any single adolescent case, there is a multiplicity of family themes and interactions, both nonverbal and verbal, that I can improvise on. Therapist creativity can only flow smoothly when we let go of our preoccupations with adhering religiously to our therapy model rules and our need to be technically precise. In the context of training therapists in brief therapy, I have frequently observed that trainees get very preoccupied with trying to come up with the "right" question or the "right" therapeutic task, at the expense of losing their creativity and sense of humor in the therapeutic process. I encourage my trainees to have fun with their clients, allow their creativity to run wild, and develop their own unique style of brief therapy, rather than try to be a clone.

My improvisational therapeutic style has been strongly influenced by the jazz saxophone greats Charlie Parker, John Coltrane, and Ornette Coleman. Parker once said, "Music is your own experience, your thoughts, your wisdom. If you don't live it, it won't come out of your horn" (Williams, 1939, p. 77). Parker had the amazing ability to "hear internally" a new harmonic conception before anybody had written it out as a formal theory (Sidran, 1971).

Coltrane viewed his music as "an instrument which can create the initial thought patterns that can change the thinking of people" (Coltrane, 1967, p. 26). His music not only had an immediate and substantial response in listeners, but, most importantly, it motivated people toward freedom (Sidran, 1971). Coltrane reached beyond the traditional harmonic conventions to find new directions to take a melodic line, new ways to free himself from the constraints presented by the structure of a tune (Fuller, 1992).

Ornette Coleman, considered to be one of the fathers of the avant-garde jazz movement, totally dispensed with the Western musical idea of harmonic structure. Coleman described his free style of horn playing in the following way (Hentoff, 1958):

> One day music will be a lot freer. Then the pattern for the tune will be forgotten and the tune itself will be the pattern, and won't have to be forced into conventional patterns. The creation of music is just as natural as the air we breathe. I believe music is really a free thing, and any way you can enjoy it you should.

All three of these jazz innovators trusted their intuitions, were risk-takers, and refused to be governed by traditional rules of musical theory. Through allowing themselves to play with total freedom, they liberated listeners from being bogged down by the familiar and opened the door for rapid changes in listeners' thinking and feeling. They essentially used themselves as "second-order" change agents (Watzlawick et al., 1974). By utilizing the improvisational methods described above, brief therapists will find themselves being more creative, having more fun, and coproducing more meaningful changes with difficult adolescents and their families than ever before.

INTEGRATION OF IDEAS FROM MICHAEL WHITE

The Australian family therapist Michael White has made many important contributions to the family therapy field (White, 1984, 1985, 1986, 1987, 1988a, 1988b; White & Epston, 1990). White's original therapeutic work was heavily based on Bateson's theoretical ideas regarding restraints and double description (White, 1986). White developed several different types of therapeutic questions to assist families in challenging the influence of restraints on their lives and to open up space for family members to view their problem situations differently. His most innovative therapeutic idea is the "externalization of the problem" (White & Epston, 1990). Through careful use of the family members' language and beliefs about the presenting problem, the problem is redefined by the therapist into an objectified external tyrant oppressing the family, including the identified client. For example, if all family members are referring to Mary's (identified client) problem as a "depression," the therapist may ask the following externalizing questions: "How long has the 'depression' been pushing all of you around?"; "Mary, when the 'depression' is trying to get the best of you, what kinds of things do your parents do to help you stand up to it?" It has been my clinical experience, with some highly entrenched adolescent cases, that these families have a strong need to talk about their longstanding oppression by the problem and typically do not respond well to Solution-Oriented questioning alone (Todd & Selekman, 1991). Externalizing the problem can be a useful therapeutic option once the brief therapist has exhausted the possibilities with the basic Solution-Oriented Brief Therapy approach.

Two other useful categories of therapeutic questions developed by White (1988) are "unique account" and "unique redescription" questions. These questions invite family members to ascribe new meaning to the exceptions they report occurring within their situation. When paired up with exception questions (de Shazer, 1988; O'Hanlon & Weiner-Davis, 1989), the "unique account" and "unique redescription" questions further amplify the family members' new perceptions about themselves and their relationships and thus make these exception experiences more meaningful for them. Some examples of "unique account" and "unique redescription" questions are as follows: "How did you manage to take this important step to turn things around?" "What were you telling yourself to get ready for this big 'responsible' step?"; "What does this tell you about yourself that is important for you to know?" "What new picture do you have of yourself as a parent that you would want others to know?"

White and Epston (1990) and Durrant and Coles (1991) like to celebrate families' victories over their oppressive problems by giving them parties, certificates, ribbons, and trophies. This end-of-therapy ritual empowers the family to continue pioneering a new direction with their lives. Therapeutic use of end-of-therapy rituals, such as throwing parties and giving awards, can nicely complement the positive and strength-based Solution-Oriented Brief Therapy approach.

INTEGRATION OF IDEAS FROM THE GALVESTON TEAM AND TOM ANDERSEN

The pioneering narrative-based family therapy approaches of the Galveston team and Tom Andersen have had a major influence on the clinical work that I do with difficult adolescents and their families. The Galveston team and Tom Andersen have both developed highly respectful, collaborative, and less interventionistic approaches to family therapy and consultation with helping professionals from larger systems (Andersen, 1987, 1991; Anderson & Goolishian, 1988a, 1988b, 1991a, 1991b; Lussardi & Miller, 1991). For these theorists, problems exist in the linguistic domain and are an "ecology of ideas" (Bogdan, 1984), therapeutic questions and new ideas are offered to clients from a position of "not knowing" and uncertainty (Andersen, 1991; Anderson & Goolishian, 1988a, 1991b) and the consultation team behind the one-way mirror is no longer presented to clients as a hidden group of privileged experts that is going to tell the interviewing therapist and family what to do or how to change.

Andersen (1991) has his consultation team switch rooms with the family and interviewing therapist midway through the therapy session to reflect on the family's dilemma. Following the team's reflections, the interviewing therapist and the family switch rooms again and the clients are invited to reflect on the team's reflections. If the consultation team has provided the family with constructions of the problem situation that come close to fitting or are acceptable to the family's beliefs, this can open up space for new possibilities and lead to "news of a difference" (Bateson, 1972) that makes a difference for them.

When utilizing a reflecting team format, I have found that it is not always necessary to offer the family a therapeutic task at the end of the session because the team's reflections have produced changes in the family's beliefs about their problem situation. Because there is a recursive relationship between family beliefs and behavior, a change in an outmoded belief system can alter the problem patterns of behavior. However, after processing the team's reflections with the family, I will explore with them whether they would like a homework assignment or not. If a homework assignment is requested, I will take a minibreak to have the team come into the room to design or select an appropriate therapeutic task. In some cases, there may be more than one useful task that would fit with the family's cooperative style and problem situation. We will then present to the family the two different tasks and allow them to choose the task they would like to try out as an experiment. Thus, therapy is collaborative in the truest sense of the word.

With some traumatized and chronic family cases, the basic Solution-Oriented Brief Therapy approach alone fails to produce changes and differences that make a difference to the family. These families may have long stories to tell about past painful events and negative experiences with former therapists and representatives from larger systems, which should not be edited by the Solution-Oriented therapist. By therapeutically focusing only on exception patterns and on altering problematic behaviors with these families, the therapist fails to remove constraints (Breunlin, Schwartz, & MacKune-Karrer, 1992) that may exist on the affective and meaning levels for family members, which prevent change from occurring. Conversational questions (Anderson & Goolishian, 1988b), which are asked from a position of "not-knowing," can open the door for family members to feel safe to disclose the "not yet said" (Anderson & Goolishian, 1988a), and can remove the constraints on the affective and meaning levels for these family members. Once the family constraints are removed, new meaning and narratives can be generated, which can lead to dramatic family changes.

BRIEF THERAPIST AS COLLABORATOR WITH LARGER SYSTEMS

Very little has been written in the brief therapy literature on how to work collaboratively with involved helpers from larger systems (Weakland & Jordan, 1990). With many of the difficult adolescent cases I have worked with, there have been multiple helpers involved, representing the juvenile justice system, schools, drug-rehabilitation programs, psychiatric hospitals, and in some cases, the child protection system. The brief therapist cannot simply intervene with just the adolescent's family and assume that therapeutic changes will be noticed by the involved helpers, who are themselves very much a part of the problem system.

Whenever I am referred a case in which there are multiple helpers actively involved, I like to conduct a macrosystemic assessment (Black, 1988; Coppersmith, 1985; Selekman & Todd, 1991) with the family to find out from them who comprises the problem-system membership and needs to be included in future therapy meetings. The problem system consists of all those individuals involved in identifying a problem and trying to solve it (Goolishian & Anderson, 1981). Once the key members of the problem system have been mobilized for the family–multiple helper meetings, they will have ample opportunities to notice changes and hear the problem being communicated about differently (Anderson, Goolishian, Pulliam, & Winderman, 1986). The family–multiple helper meetings can not only empower families, but also generate quite dramatic and rapid therapeutic changes.

When it is not possible to include some of the key members of the family–multiple helper problem system for scheduled office meetings, I will then schedule separate appointments with these helpers in their own work contexts to hear their concerns and treatment expectations and to welcome their collaboration with my cases. Oftentimes, these involved helpers greatly appreciate the fact that I take the time to meet with them on their own turf, which in itself can foster cooperative working relationships. Working collaboratively with helpers from larger systems can be an enriching learning experience for brief therapists, in that the team work can generate multiple possibilities for challenging and stuck adolescent cases.

ANATOMY OF THE "DIFFICULT" ADOLESCENT CASE

Over the past decade, I have treated and consulted on a number of adolescent cases that had been labeled by former therapists and referral sources as "difficult," "resistant," and "unmotivated." The families had been called "enmeshed," "chaotic," "crazy," "chemically dependent," and "multiproblem." Many of these youths had had multiple therapy failures in a variety of treatment settings and presented for brief therapy with such problems as substance abuse, eating disorders, self-mutilative behavior, delinquency, violent behavior, depression, and school difficulties. In repectfully listening to the stories of these adolescents and their families about their past experiences with former therapists and involved helpers from larger systems, two common themes have emerged: (1) the labels given to the adolescents and their families had a stigmatizing effect and made their situations worse, and (2) the treatment experiences were "more of the same" (Watzlawick et al., 1974) in terms of treatment variety, which exacerbated the presenting problems. I will now elaborate on how these two elements contribute to the maintenance of the identified difficult adolescents' behaviors and their families' continued involvement with mental health and addiction professionals.

LABELS CREATE A THERAPEUTIC "BLACK HOLE"

In thinking about the various oppressive and stigmatizing labels difficult adolescent clients tend to be given while on tour through the mental health and chemical-dependency treatment delivery systems, I am reminded of the poignant words of family therapy pioneer Harry Goolishian. Regarding the "deficiency language" mental health professionals have utilized with clients over the last century, he said (Goolishian, 1991):

> The deficiency language has created a world of description that understands only through what is wrong, broken, absent, or insufficient. This deficiency language has created a world of mental health that can be compared to a black hole out of which there is little hope to escape whether we are a clinician, theoretician, or researcher. In using the metaphor of the black hole, I am trying to capture the essence of a system of meaning whose forces are so strong that it is impossible to escape out of the system and into other realities. (pp. 1–2)

One powerful written work that has perpetuated the mental health "black hole" is the third revised edition of the *Di-*

agnostic and Statistical Manual of Mental Disorders (DSM-III-R; American Psychiatric Association, 1987). Tomm (1990) contends there is no empirical support for the labels used in the DSM-III-R nor any provision for interpersonal, familial, cultural, or institutional diagnoses. Clients are pathologized through labeling, totalizing, and segregating. On a pragmatic level, the DSM-III-R offers little to therapists in the way of formulating treatment plans. In his plea for revamping the DSM-III-R, Wolin (1991) suggests that this volume should contain a listing of client strengths as long and as technical as the diseases and disorders described within it.

The popular "recovery movement," which is based on the philosophy of Alcoholics' Anonymous and the disease model of addiction, has extended its deficiency language to every possible human behavior, such as eating, sex, and exercise (Peele, 1989). Disease model theorists tend to believe that the majority of youths living with an alcoholic parent will most likely become "emotional cripples" for life (Wolin, 1991). Their only hope of recovery is through their active participation in Al-Ateen, Al-Anon, and Adult Children of Alcoholics' groups. The recovery movement literature fails to identify children of alcoholics' strengths, resiliency, and specific competency areas (Wolin, 1991). What do tend to be described in this literature, which is quite alarming to parents, are all of the negative traits children of alcoholics are supposed to have, particularly the high risk for developing alcohol or drug problems (Katz & Liu, 1991). Selekman and Todd (1991) have worked with numerous adolescent cases in which parental indoctrination to the recovery movement lifestyle and constant preoccupation with their adolescent's future use of alcohol or drugs ended up creating self-fulfilling prophecies.

Once an adolescent is identified as being a substance abuser, he or she will most likely be referred to an outpatient or inpatient chemical dependency program whose treatment philosophy is based on AA and the disease model. There the adolescent will be prompted to admit to being either an "alcoholic" or a "drug addict." If the adolescent refuses to admit to being one or the other, the treatment team will confront him or her on his or her "denial." Many of these chemical dependency programs provide "assembly line" treatment, which usually takes the form of total abstinence treatment goals, self-help groups, education, and family supportive counseling (Selekman & Todd, 1991). Perceived choice is not encouraged in a system where adolescents are coerced to take a particular course of action, or in programs where a relatively standard treatment is provided for all clients (Orford & Hawker, 1974). Three major reasons why this heavy-handed treatment strategy does not work with substance-abusing adolescents are: (1) adolescent drug users rarely accept labels of "addiction," "alcoholic," and "addict" (Glassner & Loughlin, 1987); (2) adolescent drug users tend to view their chemical use as a normative social behavior that they will outgrow in adulthood (Glassner & Loughlin, 1987); and (3) research indicates that when alcohol abusers receive a confrontational therapy approach, they show much higher levels of resistance and negative treatment outcomes (Miller & Sovereign, 1989; Patterson & Forgatch, 1985). One treatment outcome study found that more than 50% of the substance-abusing youth who had received traditional inpatient chemical dependency treatment returned to problem use patterns following discharge (Harrison & Hoffman, 1987). More recently, follow-up studies have indicated that posttreatment relapse rates for adolescents are reportedly as high as 85% (Dembo, 1992).

Despite my qualms about the recovery movement and the use of the disease model with adolescents, I do believe strongly in utilizing self-help groups when clients are looking for further support outside of therapy sessions. I view their prior and concurrent involvement in Al-Anon or other self-help groups as a strength and a sign of their resourcefulness. I do not, however, take a shotgun approach regarding family members' immediate participation in self-help groups at the beginning of treatment. Similarly, I do not demand immediate abstinence from chemical use with adolescents before I will work with them. With regular and heavy adolescent substance abusers, cutting back has proven to be a much more palatable initial treatment goal (Selekman & Todd, 1991). I will, however, pursue total abstinence treatment goals with adolescents that are experiencing severe physical complications from their heavy alcohol or substance abuse. Periodic use of outpatient or inpatient detoxification can also be useful for disrupting self-destructive cycles of heavy substance abuse.

"MORE OF THE SAME" TREATMENT VARIETY

The average difficult adolescent case has been through two or more past treatment experiences that usually took the form of "more of the same" (Watzlawick et al., 1974) type of therapy or treatment setting. As the treatment failures pile up, the adolescent's symptoms become more entrenched and chronic, which may trigger vicious guilt/blame cycles of interaction within the family (Selekman, 1989). Frequently, difficult adolescent clients and their families have shared with me that they had very little input in their past treatment experiences, in terms of deciding the goals for treatment and being actively involved in treatment planning. With some residential and hospital-based treatment experiences, former adolescent clients of mine reported that the treatment team failed to impact any significant changes with their families. Even when family therapy was utilized, some difficult adolescent clients told me that most of the therapeutic work was with the parents and that the adolescent's individual goals or expectations were not addressed. Another commonality of past treatment experiences was the failure to include the involved helpers from larger systems in the treatment process.

Difficult adolescents and their families do not have to be hard to treat if there is a conscious effort with each new case to: (1) avoid the use of labeling; (2) expect that clients have the strengths and resources to change; (3) view therapy as a collaborative enterprise in which clients determine the goals for treatment; (4) find out what clients liked and disliked about former therapy experiences; (5) give the adolescent individual session time to assess his or her needs, goals, and expectations; (6) actively involve concerned helpers from larger systems, and (7) be therapeutically flexible and improvise when necessary. Throughout the years, clients have taught me these valuable therapeutic lessons, which have helped me grow as a therapist and be a more effective helper. As brief therapists, we need to avoid adopting a priviliged expert position, and instead serve as consulting coauthors to clients by helping them rewrite more satisfactory stories.

T W O

GUIDING ASSUMPTIONS
WITH AN EYE ON SOLUTIONS

I n this chapter I will present 10 useful Solution-Oriented
assumptions. The assumptions are highly pragmatic and
offer therapists a new lens for viewing the difficult adolescent case. Each of the guiding assumptions provides a wellness perspective on adolescent problems, families, and brief
therapy.

ASSUMPTION 1: Resistance is not a useful concept.

The traditional psychotherapeutic concept of *resistance* is an
unhelpful idea that has handicapped therapists (de Shazer,
1984). It implies that the client does not want to change and the
therapist is separate from the client system he or she is treating.
De Shazer (1982, 1984) has argued convincingly for therapists
to approach each new client case from a position of therapist–
client cooperation, rather than focusing on resistance, power,
and control. As therapists, we are observing ourselves in relation to the client systems we are treating. We can never find an
outside place from which to observe our clients (Hoffman,
1988). According to de Shazer (1982):

> Each family (individual or couple) shows an unique way of attempt-
> ing to cooperate and the therapist's job becomes, first, to describe
> that particular manner to himself that the family shows and, then, to

cooperate with the family's way and thus, to promote change. (pp. 9–10)

Like Columbo, the detective, we need to listen and observe carefully to find clues that help identify our clients' unique cooperative response patterns. These clues take the form of how family members respond to our questions verbally and nonverbally, as well as by the way they manage therapeutic tasks between sessions. Once important clues have been discovered, the therapist should continue to match the questions and therapeutic tasks with the family's unique way of cooperating. For example, if a parent is highly pessimistic about a daughter's delinquent behavior ever changing, the therapist should assume an equally pessimistic stance, particularly if previous attempts to have the mother identify nonproblem patterns of behavior (exceptions) or hypothetical future solutions proved to be futile. The therapist could ask the following questions: "How come things are not worse with your daughter?"; "What steps are you taking to prevent things from getting worse?" If a family is given a therapeutic task and they modify it, this helpful clue tells the therapist that future tasks need to be modifiable for this particular family.

Erickson (Gordon & Meyers-Anderson, 1981) shared a wonderful story with his hypnotherapist trainees that captures the essence of the cooperation principle:

> I was returning from high school one day and a runaway horse with his bridle on sped past a group of us into a farmer's yard, looking for a drink of water. I hopped on the horse's back . . . since he had a bridle on, I managed to take hold of the tick rein and said "Giddy up!" . . . headed for the highway. I knew the horse would turn in the right direction . . . I didn't know what the right direction was. And the horse trotted and galloped along. Now and then he would forget he was on the highway and start into a field. So I would pull on him a bit and call his attention to the fact the highway was where he was supposed to be. And finally, about four miles from where I boarded him, he turned into a farm yard and the farmer said, "So that's how that critter came back! Where did you find him?" I said, "About

four miles from here." "How did you know you should come here?" I said, "I didn't know, the horse knew . . . all I did was keep his attention on the road." (p. 166)

For Erickson, the horse story served as a great metaphor for how therapists should conduct therapy. Young Erickson's experience teaches us that it is easier to ride the horse in the direction that it wants to go.

ASSUMPTION 2: Cooperation is inevitable.

Besides carefully matching our questions and therapeutic tasks with our clients' unique cooperative response patterns, there are several important rapport-building tools that therapists can utilize to further enhance the cooperation process. Therapists can first and foremost utilize whatever their clients bring to therapy—their strengths and resources, key client words and belief system material, as well as nonverbal behaviors (Gordon & Meyers-Anderson, 1981; de Shazer, 1985). The following case example demonstrates the efficacy of the utilization strategy.

> Joe, a single parent, brought his two adolescent children for therapy due to their stealing, lying, and failure to follow his "household rules." Joe had grown up in an "alcoholic family" and the childrens' mother was an "alcoholic." Joe and his ex-wife had been divorced for 5 years. Joe attended "seven Al-Anon meetings every week" and demanded that his two children also "work their own recovery programs" by regularly attending "Al-Ateen." The more Joe would force his children to go to Al-Ateen, the more they would resist, steal, lie, and not follow his rules. In an attempt to disrupt this repetitive pattern of interaction, I shared with Joe that I had recently heard about a study at a big name university that actually demonstrated that it is possible to "enable" your children to engage in "children of alcoholics" behaviors like "stealing and lying," and what he needed to do is "detach with love." Once Joe began detaching from his children regarding demanding their involvement in Al-Ateen, the children not only stopped acting out, but they

would spontaneously surprise him by occasionally asking to be taken to Al-Ateen meetings.

With Joe's case, I had successfully utilized key client language and belief material from Joe's many years of involvement in Al-Anon to cocreate a new construction of Joe's problem situation, a frame that was more acceptable to his worldview. Once Joe's thinking changed about how he viewed the problem, his parental behavior dramatically changed as well.

TOOLS FOR FOSTERING COOPERATION

Positive relabeling is another useful therapeutic tool that can foster a cooperative climate and reduce client defensiveness (Barton & Alexander, 1981). An angry parent's behavior can be positively relabeled by the therapist as demonstrating a high level of concern and commitment towards resolving the presenting problem. A withdrawn adolescent can be positively relabeled as being a thoughtful adolescent.

Other useful rapport-building tools for fostering therapist–client cooperation are purposive use of self-disclosure, the use of humor, normalizing, demonstrating cultural and gender sensitivity, and therapeutic compliments. Mark Twain once said, "Against the assault of laughter nothing can stand." Humor can reduce tension, distance the client from his or her concerns, and heal those in pain. Madanes (1984) contends that "what makes change possible is the therapist's ability to be optimistic and to see what is funny or appealing in a grim situation" (p. 137).

Family life-cycle changes and normative crises can contribute to the development of adolescent and family difficulties. By normalizing these difficulties, family members can be put at ease and begin to entertain new ways of looking at their problem situation. For example, I frequently normalize for parents the adolescent rebellious behavior, drug experimentation, and acting-out behavior that may follow a parental divorce.

Finally, I like to compliment each family member on the various coping strategies and productive steps they have taken toward resolving the presenting problem. Therapeutic compliments and cheerleading (de Shazer, 1985, 1988) empower clients by providing them with positive reinforcement for their creative problem-solving efforts. Each compliment is carefully interspersed with key client words, belief system material, or positively relabeled negative behavior. Both the compliments and the intervention designed or selected for a particular family grow out of the interviewing process. Typically, the compliments are constructed by the therapist during his or her intersession break 15 minutes before the conclusion of the therapy session. However, I also like to give spontaneous in-session compliments to family members as well. These in-session compliments may take the form of "high fives" for adolescents who have taken responsible steps prior to entering treatment or during the course of therapy. With parents, I may give handshakes to further reinforce their productive problem-solving efforts as well. The "high fives" and handshakes are useful in conjunction with other cheerleading responses by the therapist. The therapist can respond to client exceptions with: "Wow! How did you do that!?"; "How did you come up with that idea!?" "How" questions have clients compliment themselves on their resourcefulness.

During the therapist consultation break, the clients, while waiting in the lobby area, are often anticipating a "doom and gloom" presentation by the therapist. Parents who have already experienced failure in therapy typically assume that they will be blamed for their adolescents' problems. The adolescent clients may anticipate that they will be blamed for the family problems or that an argument will erupt when the session is reconvened. Much to each family members' surprise, the therapist delivers an empowering message of hope and encouragement to the family, thus heightening motivation and commitment to the therapeutic process. Well-constructed compliments can produce head nods or "yes-set" hypnotic responses (de Shazer, 1985) from family members. These nonverbal hypnotic responses indicate that the compliments are either acceptable to or come close to fitting family members' beliefs about their situation and will most likely lead to the family's compliance with the assigned therapeutic task. For example, the therapist compliments a mother for bringing her first-time court-involved son to therapy in an effort to take "preventative measures," thereby preventing his legal difficulties from escalating into a future incarceration. The son in this case would be complimented for "showing up" for the session and being "responsible."

ASSUMPTION 3: Change is inevitable.

Buddhists have professed for centuries that change is a continuous process and that stability is an illusion (Mitchell, 1988). If you expect that change will occur with your clients, your expectancy of change will influence their behavior. The therapist's belief in the client's ability to change can be a significant determinant of treatment outcome (Leake & King, 1977). Motivational researchers have found that one of the most important factors with motivated subjects is their self-perception that they are in fact doing well with task assignments (Peters & Waterman, 1982). Jones (1977) studied two groups of adults that were given the same 10 puzzles to solve. After having the subjects turn in their puzzles for scoring, half of the subjects were told that they did well on the puzzles, whereas the other half of the subjects were told they did poorly. The group of subjects were then given another 10 puzzles to solve. The half of the subjects that were told that they had fared well on the first set of puzzles ended up doing much better on the second set than did the other group. Similar studies have been conducted in the school context. One study demonstrated that when teachers believed that their students would do well on an IQ test, those students scored 25 points higher on their tests than other students with different teachers (Bennis, 1976).

In the context of brief therapy, it is helpful to think *when* change *will* occur with our clients, rather than *if* it will happen. We need to cocreate positive self-fulfilling prophecies with our clients. Gingerich and his colleagues (1988) have demonstrated in their interviewing research that there is a direct relationship between therapist "change talk" and positive treatment outcomes. The "change talk" therapists in the study utilized presuppositional language such as "when" and "will," rather than "if" and "would," and they spent the majority of their session time having clients talk about past, present, and future successes. The "problem talk" therapists, on the other hand, were lost in a sea of information about past and present problems. The "problem talk" cases tended to have negative treatment outcomes. There is sound empirical support for the deleterious effects of having clients work through their "bad" feelings in therapy. Snyder and White (1982) demonstrated in their study that depressed subjects tended to get more depressed when asked to talk about painful past events and encouraged to try and better understand their depression. The Milan Associates, in their clinical research with schizophrenics and their families, have observed that change cannot occur under a negative connotation (Boscolo, Cecchin, Hoffman, & Penn, 1987).

In keeping with the Milan Associates position on how change occurs, one important way therapists can cocreate a context for change with families is through the use of humor and playfulness. Getting family members to laugh in each other's company can help them experience themselves together in a new way, which can open up the door for change.

ASSUMPTION 4: Only a small change is necessary.

Erickson believed that small changes will snowball into bigger changes (Gordon & Meyers-Anderson, 1981). Once clients are encouraged to value minimal changes, they are more likely to expect to make further changes. The Buddhist Lao-tzu believed strongly in this approach to problem solving, and he wrote, "Act without doing; work without effort. Think of the small as large and the few as many. Confront the difficult while it is still easy; accomplish the great task by a series of small acts" (Mitchell, 1988, p. 63).

All parts of a family system are interconnected in such a way that a small change in one part of the system can ripple on and cause changes in the other parts. Szapocznik and his colleagues (Szapocznik, Kurtines, Foote, Perez-Vidal, & Hervis, 1983, 1986), in their study for the National Institute on Drug Abuse, provided some empirical grounding for the idea that small changes can lead to system-wide changes in the family. The researchers had two groups of subjects; one group consisted only of the adolescent drug abusers, whereas the other group consisted of the drug abusers and their families. Both groups received a Brief Strategic Family Therapy treatment. Szapocznik and his colleagues found that the one-person group fared equally well on all treatment measures up to 3 years follow-up. Two important findings came out of this study: (1) it is possible to change an entire family system through one individual family member, and (2) it is not necessary to engage all family members for treatment in order to change the identified client. The latter finding challenges the longstanding family therapy rubric that all family members living under the same roof need to be engaged for treatment in order to change the identified client. Along these same lines, I have found it helpful to keep things simple and begin treatment with the nucleus of family members that present themselves for therapy. This is also another way to foster therapist–client cooperation.

ASSUMPTION 5: Clients have the strengths and resources to change.

Recently, *American Health* magazine conducted a large, nationwide Gallup Poll that surveyed how people best solve their problems. The vast majority of the people interviewed indicated that they were 10 times more likely to change on their own without the help of doctors, therapists, and self-help groups. Of the individuals surveyed, 30% reported that positive feelings, desires, and simply the recognition that the time has come for a big change were the motivating forces for them to give up such tenacious habits as cigarette smoking, overeating, and excessive drinking (Gurin, 1990). One of the most surprising findings was that only 3% of the time did doctors help these people change, whereas psychologists, psychiatrists, and self-help groups got even less credit for personal changes. Family and close friends were ranked as providing the most support in helping with change (Gurin, 1990).

As the *American Health* survey demonstrates, all clients have strengths and resources that therapists can capitalize on in the co-construction of solutions. Any past successes that clients have had can serve as models for present and future successes. Clients are more likely to cooperate and change in a therapeutic context that accentuates their strengths and resourcefulness, rather than one that focuses on problems and pathology. Beavers and Hampson (1990) found in their family therapy research that therapies that emphasize the power of families, in possessing the strengths and resources to solve their problems, tend to produce better outcome results than other therapies.

DeFrain and Stinnett (1992) have developed a family wellness therapy approach based on their 16 years of researching what they called "strong families." These researchers elicited the subjects' expertise by asking such questions as: "What are the strengths of your family?" and "What are areas of potential growth?" Based on the answers to the above questions, they discovered six major qualities that these families possessed: (1) commitment; (2) appreciation and affection; (3) positive communication; (4) time together; (5) spiritual well-being; and (6) the ability to cope with stress and crisis. According to DeFrain and Stinnett (1992), "strong families are optimistic in the face of adversity and tend to view a crisis situation as being both a challenge and an opportunity for growth" (p. 22). Recently, these researchers demonstrated that their family wellness approach can be quite effective in improving family functioning with child abuse and domestic violence cases.

Wolin (1991) has also empirically demonstrated that individuals growing up in high-stress family environments can be "emboldened by adversity." Over a 20-year period, Wolin and his colleagues studied a large group of children of alcoholics. Of the sample, 85% grew up to become well-functioning adults. Wolin (1991) attributes the subjects' success to personal resilience and pride. Ground-breaking research such as Wolin's helps challenge the popular belief that children of alcoholics will grow up to become emotionally flawed adults.

With difficult adolescent clients, I have found it quite useful to place the adolescent in the position of an expert by asking him or her the following questions: "If I were to work with other teenagers just like you, what advice would you give me to help them out?"; "What should I not do with them?"; "What kinds of things should I do with them as a counselor?"; "What kinds of things should I ask them about?" These types of open-ended questions can elicit the adolescent's strengths and expertise, help foster a cooperative relationship, and offer the therapist invaluable wisdom about helpful strategies for engaging and treating adolescents.

Another useful therapeutic strategy for capitalizing on the adolescents' expertise is to channel his or her strengths into the problem area. The following case example (from Selekman, 1989a) best exemplifies this therapeutic strategy.

Robert and his mother pursued family therapy with the author because the former was heavily abusing alcohol. The mother was convinced that her son was an "alcoholic just like his father and grandfather." In the first interview, I discovered that Robert was a former "state wrestling champion" for his high school. I took a strong interest in Robert's wrestling abilities and inquired about his past "training regime." Throughout the interview, both the mother and Robert boasted about the latter's past illustrious wrestling career. However, the mother was quite worried that "the death grip of alcoholism was trying to claim Robert's life." Alcoholism was being described by the family as being a three-generational oppressive monster! I decided to externalize (White & Epston, 1990) the alcoholism problem into the "Alcohol Monster." Sensing the family's love for wrestling and desire to conquer the Alcohol Monster, I developed a wrestling ritual using the wrestling scoring system: one point was an escape; two points was a reversal; and three points was a near pin. The family came up with their own scoring criterion—that is, Robert would receive three points from his coach (mother) if he would drink a soda, rather than a beer with friends. At the end of each day, Robert was to report to his mother how well he scored in standing up to the Alcohol Monster. After three therapy sessions over a 2-month period, Robert and his mother had successfully pinned the Alcohol Monster. In fact, Robert rejoined his school wrestling team for his senior year and sported a 16–4 record.

Carl Hammerschlag, in his book *The Dancing Healers: A Doctor's Journey of Healing with Native Americans,* shares with readers a valuable and humbling learning experience he had had as a psychiatrist while treating a Pueblo priest and clan chief named Santiago. Santiago had been admitted into Hammerschlag's hospital dying from congestive heart failure. Upon meeting Santiago for the first time, Hammerschlag was asked by the priest: "Where did you learn to heal?" Hammerschlag quickly reeled off all of his many academic credentials. Santiago then asked: "Do you know how to dance?" Hammerschlag began to dance by Santiago's bedside. Santiago started laughing, got out of bed, and showed Hammerschlag how to dance. Santiago then asked: "You must be able to dance if you are to heal people." Hammerschlag then asked: "And will you teach me your steps?" Santiago replied: "Yes, I can teach you my steps, but you will have to hear your own music" (Hammerschlag, 1988, pp. 9–10).

ASSUMPTION 6: Problems are unsuccessful attempts to resolve difficulties.

The MRI theorists (Watzlawick et al., 1974) built their Brief Problem-Focused Therapy approach around the assumption that it is the client's attempted solution that is the problem. Family members are stuck viewing the problem in one particular way and engaging in the same repetitive patterns of interactions around the identified client. I like to share with parents that problems are like quicksand. The more they worry about them and frantically try to do something about them, the more they get swallowed up by them. For some parents of acting-out adolescents, it is helpful to interpret for them their problem-maintaining interaction patterns with their adolescents. I will point out to them that the more super-responsible they are in relationship to their adolescent, the more super-irresponsible he or she will be. According to the MRI theorists, (Watzlawick et al., 1974) there are three common ways clients mishandle their difficulties:

1. Action is necessary but is not taken.
2. Action is taken when it should not be.
3. Action is taken at the wrong logical level.

The first way of mishandling a problem is to behave as if it does not exist. By denying or minimizing the problem, any attempted solution to remedy the situation is perceived as being unnecessary. Thus, the problem becomes greatly compounded by the "problems" created through its mishandling (Watzlawick et al., 1974). The second type of mishandling has as its central theme the refusal to accept any proposed solution other than one based on a Utopian belief that things "should be" a certain way, thus making the idea of going for small therapeutic changes an impossibility (Bodin, 1981). The Utopian extremist approach can frequently be seen with parents placing their rebellious acting-out adolescents in an inpatient psychiatric facility. Finally, the third type of mishandling takes the form of a "be spontaneous!" paradox (Watzlawick et al., 1974). For example, the more a father demands that his 16-year-old son be more affectionate towards his mother, the more the son fails because affection is a spontaneous behavior and cannot be forced.

The more restrained or stuck a family is in viewing their problem situation, the harder it is for new information to get into the system in order to alter outmoded beliefs and to change behavior. With chronic adolescent cases, the exceptions or non-problem patterns of behavior often go unnoticed by family members and therapists because they do not fit with the "dominant story" (White & Epston, 1990).

With families that have had multiple past treatment experiences, it is important to inquire as to what family members liked and disliked about former therapists. I once worked with a 16-year-old chronic runaway case that had had 16 therapy experiences in every type of treatment setting. This case exemplifies the importance of exploring past therapists' attempted solutions with a family.

Bonnie had been heavily abusing drugs and running away from state to state for 5 years. She had graduated from juvenile probation to adult parole status. Her mother was a recovering alcoholic and drug addict. The mother had been married five times and was quite happy with her fifth husband. In the first interview, I asked the family what they did not like with their former therapists. The mother disclosed a recent negative experience she had had with a structural family therapist. The therapist had apparently balked at the mother's suggestion about having the stepfather serve as an active disciplinarian with her in a team effort. Bonnie shared with me that she gets "real mad" when therapists "side up" with her parents "against" her. This information proved to be quite useful to me, in that I needed to operate differently as a therapist with Bonnie's family. For instance, I encouraged parental team work and gave Bonnie individual session time in the context of the family therapy sessions.

AVOIDING "MORE OF THE SAME"

Besides exploring past attempted parental and therapist solutions, the therapist needs to be cognizant of what he or she might be doing in treatment with a current case that might be "more of the same" (Watzlawick et al., 1974). Oftentimes when a therapist is feeling stuck, he or she might be asking questions and giving therapeutic tasks that may have already proved to be futile in earlier sessions, or are too similar to what the parents have already tried in the past. When I'm feeling stuck with a particular family case, this is a signal to me that therapeutic improvisation is necessary. Therapeutic improvisation may take the form of storytelling, using humor, utilizing a therapeutic technique or task from a different therapy model, doing something dramatic, or changing the therapy context in some way, such as adding a reflecting team when working solo, changing the appointment time or day, or rearranging the office.

Outside of the therapy room, the therapist has to work collaboratively with the referring person and other involved helpers to negotiate realistic treatment goals for cases and maximize opportunities for them to notice changes in the identified client. In Chapter 5, I will discuss this strategy in more detail.

Einstein believed that it is impossible to solve a problem with the same kind of thinking that created the problem. Solutions require a type of thinking and action outside the original problem explanations and problem-solving efforts.

ASSUMPTION 7: You do not need to know a great deal about the problem in order to solve it.

No problem happens all of the time; there may be hours, days, sometimes weeks when the identified client and her family are not being pushed around by the problem. With the analytic attention of a Sherlock Holmes, the therapist needs to investigate in great detail with each family member what they are doing differently during these nonproblem times.

In fact, often clients are well on their way to solving their problems before entering the therapy arena. Weiner-Davis and her colleagues (Weiner-Davis et al., 1987) found in their research that two-thirds of their sample had already taken some helpful steps towards resolving their presenting problems between the time of the phone call to the agency and the first session. I have conducted a similar study out of my clinic in which each caller at intake was given a modified version of de Shazer's "formula first session task" (de Shazer, 1985). The intake specialist would give the calling parent the following task on the telephone prior to the initial therapy session:

> "In order to better assist your therapist with knowing what your family strengths are, we would like you to notice what is happening in your relationship with your son/daughter that you would like to continue to have happen. You can make mental notes or write those things down."

The exploratory study produced some interesting clinical results. With some cases, parents would cancel their initial therapy session appointments and leave such messages as: "I realized that things aren't that bad"; "I have a good relationship with my son"; "I want to hold off for a while." The majority of the cases involved with the research project ended up being one, two, or three session therapies. Many of the clients brought in long lists of "good things" that were already happening in their families. The therapists' main job with these cases was simply to capitalize on what was already working for the families by amplifying and consolidating pretreatment gains.

When exploring with family members about their exceptions, I not only ask questions about useful things they are doing, but also inquire about helpful self-talk. Self-talk consists of useful tapes that family members play in their heads in helping them stand up to the problem. For example, I may ask an adolescent with anger management problems: "What do you tell yourself to avoid allowing the anger to get the best of you?"; "What tape do you play in your head to help you stand up to the anger?" The audiotape metaphor is particularly useful with adolescents.

Once important exception sequences of behavior and useful client self-talk have been identified, the therapist's job is to amplify this material through cheerleading, highlighting differences, and moving the clients into the future with presuppositional questions (O'Hanlon & Weiner-Davis, 1989). With some cases, I may bring out my trusty imaginary crystal ball (de Shazer, 1985) and have family members discuss in great detail what further family changes they will see 2 to 3 weeks down the road, through the crystal ball. The exceptions elicited by the therapist can serve as building blocks towards co-constructing solutions with clients. When the exception descriptions are placed next to the client's problem-saturated construction of their situation, this will lead to clients making new discoveries about themselves, and to what Bateson (1972) referred to as "news of a difference that makes a difference." Because there is a recursive relationship between meaning and action, a change in the client's view of the situation may lead to a change in their behavior.

ASSUMPTION 8: Clients define the goals for treatment.

If you do not know where you are going with your clients, you will end up somewhere else (O'Hanlon & Weiner-Davis, 1989). When stuck or frustrated with a particular case, the therapist may be lost in a sea of information about problems, he or she may not know what the client's treatment goal is, or the treatment goal may be too monolithic. Our job as therapists is to negotiate solvable problems and realistic treatment goals. We cannot change a borderline adolescent, but we can alter one of the presenting symptoms, such as self-mutilative behavior. We can see behaviors and observe behavioral changes over the course of treatment. It is important for the therapist to elicit from clients a videotape description (O'Hanlon & Weiner-Davis, 1989) of how things will look when the presenting problem is solved. Ideally, the client's videotaped description will contain the "who," "what," "when," and "how" of goal attainment.

When clients present for therapy, they often reel off a long laundry list of problems that they want to see resolved. The main task of the therapist is to have the family identify the problem they want to see changed first. Once a problem is selected by the family as their initial focus of attention for treatment, the therapist needs to break down their treatment goal into something concrete, small, and changeable. For example, I once worked with a family case where the high priority for the parents was to have their substance-abusing son clean his entire bedroom in 1 week's time. The bedroom allegedly had looked "like a pigsty" for the past 5 years. The parents in this case had found petrified peanut butter and jelly sandwiches under their son's bed. Because the parent's goal was too monolithic, I encouraged them to negotiate with their son on one part of the bedroom that he would be willing to clean up in 1 week's time.

Research indicates the need for client self-determination in the therapeutic process. When clients think they have even modest personal control over their destinies, they will persist at mastering tasks, do better at managing them, and become more committed to the change process. There is empirical evidence that when clients themselves choose a course of action from among alternatives, they are more likely to adhere to it and succeed (Miller, 1985). Several studies in the addiction field have demonstrated that when clients are given a choice regarding treatment goals and the type of treatment they want to receive, they will be more motivated and have more favorable treatment outcomes (Kissen, Platz, & Su, 1971; Parker, Winstead, & Willi, 1979). Insistence on a particular treatment goal, despite the client's perceptions and wishes, can compromise motivation and treatment outcome (Sanchez-Craig & Lei, 1986; Thorton, Gottheil, Gellins, & Alterman, 1977).

ASSUMPTION 9: Reality is observer-defined and the therapist participates in cocreating the therapy system's reality.

Bateson (1972) wrote that the beliefs a person has "about what sort of world it is, will determine how he sees it and acts within it, and his ways of perceiving and acting will determine his beliefs about its nature" (p. 314). As members of the new therapist–client observing system, our constructions of the client's presenting problem will be based primarily on our own theoretical maps and personal experiences in the world (Efran & Lukens, 1985; von Foerster, 1981; Maturana & Varela, 1988). Einstein believed that it is our theories that determine what we can observe. If you are a structural family therapist, most likely you will see pathological family structures like "enmeshment" or "disengagement" (Minuchin, 1974). If you are a psychodynamically oriented therapist, you probably will see unresolved conflicts and psychic deficits. What you will see is what you will get. Therapists "cannot not have a theory" (Anderson & Goolishian, 1991b).

There is no such thing as a "God's eye" view; we can never find an objective outside place from which to look at our clients (Hoffman, 1988). The therapist and supervisor/therapeutic team are members of the new therapist–client observing problem system. We are consulting coauthors in helping our clients rewrite their problem-saturated stories. In our conversational discourse with clients, we need to interact in a way that introduces meaningful differences that can challenge outmoded beliefs and alter behavior patterns. According to Andersen (1991), there are three types of therapeutic constructions that occur in conversations with clients: (1) constructions that are "too similar" to how the clients already view their problem; (2) constructions that are perceived by the clients as being "too unusual" and are rejected or disregarded; and (3) constructions that are neither too similar nor too unusual, and can lead to a change in the client's original perceptions of their problem. The last category of therapeutic constructions can only be generated when the therapist is "staying close" to the clients in the therapeutic process. By "staying close," I mean carefully utilizing key client words and belief material, and embedding the client's presuppositional language in therapeutic questions and prescribed tasks. This can lead to the coauthoring of a solution-determined story with the family (de Shazer, 1991).

ASSUMPTION 10: There are many ways to look at a situation, none more "correct" than others.

For every event that occurs in the world, there are at least two or more explanations of that event. Bateson (1980) referred to this form of description as "double or multiple comparison" (p. 97). There are no final explanations of reality. The great surrealist artist René Magritte liked to play upon the human urge to make sense of or give definitive explanations for the images in his paintings. He once said, "Our gaze always wants to penetrate further so as to see at last the object, the reason for our existence" (Whitfield, 1992, p. 62). Many of the images found in Magritte's paintings are metaphors for the different ways in which truth and meaning remain concealed.

As therapists, we need to be careful not to become too wedded to our therapy models of choice. Emile Chartier, the French existentialist philosopher, once said, "Nothing is more dangerous than an idea when it is the only one you have." Therapeutic flexibility is essential with difficult adolescent cases. Solution-Oriented Brief Family Therapy is not a panacea for every adolescent case. When clinically necessary, I integrate ideas from other therapy approaches or abandon the Solution-Oriented Brief Family Therapy approach and try a completely different therapeutic approach.

T H R E E

THE FIRST INTERVIEW: COCREATING A CONTEXT FOR CHANGE

COCREATING A THERAPEUTIC CLIMATE FOR CHANGE

There are four important therapeutic activities in which the brief therapist must engage in so as to cocreate a climate for change with difficult adolescents and their families: (1) explaining the session format, (2) rapport-building, (3) assessing customership, and (4) purposeful systemic interviewing. After discussing these four important therapeutic activities, I will conclude the chapter with a brief overview of the mechanics of conducting the Solution-Oriented Brief Family Therapy interview and offer helpful guidelines for therapeutic task design and selection.

EXPLAINING THE SESSION FORMAT

Before beginning the rapport-building process with new clients, I like to explain the session format and see if I can secure written consent to videotape the session and also have my therapist colleagues serve as a consultation team for collaboration purposes. When describing the session format, I explain to the family that I like to spend some time with the whole group together, meet with the parents alone, and give the adolescent individual session time as well. I also tell the family that we will be taking an intersession break, at which time my colleagues will come into the therapy room and we (the family and I) will go behind the one-way mirror to listen to their reflections about the interview thus far. I explain to the family that we will then switch rooms with the team again and that the family will be invited to reflect on the team's reflections. I also point out to the family that I might invite the team to briefly come in to join us later in the session so we can brainstorm a helpful home-work assignment to offer them. When working alone, I still take a minibreak to "meet with myself" to prepare my editorial of the session and offer them a homework assignment, if requested.

With regard to my request to videotape our therapy sessions, I explain to my clients that the video camera acts as a second set of eyes and ears and it often captures important things that I missed in the session that can help me help them better. When presenting the idea of having my therapist colleagues observe and collaborate with us during our sessions, I point out to the family that "three heads are better than one" in terms of brainpower and creativity. Families have rarely turned me down with videotaping and having a consultation team observing our sessions. Sometimes a family will request that the consultation team join us in the same room. My colleagues and I have no problem honoring this request.

RAPPORT BUILDING

After explaining the session format to the family, I begin the rapport-building process. I invite each family member, begin-ning with the parents, to share with me what they do best, their personal strengths, talents, and hobbies. With parents, I am particularly interested in the type of work they do and detailed information about their strengths in their work roles. This valuable information can be useful to the brief therapist in the presenting problem area. The following case example illustrates how I utilized a parent's champion chess-playing ability to help him resolve his power struggle with his daughter.

In the very first 10 minutes of the initial session with Bob and his daughter Patricia, I discovered that the former was a world-class chess player. He had won numerous matches worldwide. While listening to Bob talk about his great chess-playing abilities, I explored with him what it was about his style of play that had made him a champion. Bob shared with me that it was "the first move" that makes the difference between winning and losing. I asked him more detailed questions about how he decides what the "first move" should be. According to Bob, he would "carefully think out different first moves" and his "opponent's counter-moves" before doing anything. This strategy had consistently worked for Bob in his chess matches. With his daughter Patricia, on the other hand, he would not carefully think through his "first move," but instead would overreact to her testy behavior by yelling and getting trapped in power struggles with her. I decided to channel Bob's chess-playing "first move" strategy into the problem area. I gave Bob the task of utilizing his "first move" chess strategy every time Patricia tried to push his buttons. Bob quickly discovered that by thinking through his "first move" with Patricia led to a decrease in his yelling, and his daughter's behavior changed.

When joining with adolescents, I like to know what grade they are in, what their favorite subjects are and why, if they play any sports, what musical groups they like, and if they have any special talents and hobbies. You don't have to like the adolescents' music, but if you know the names of the popular heavy metal and rap groups, the adolescents think you are "cool." With more streetwise youth, it is helpful to be familiar with the street lingo, particularly the street names of drugs of abuse and drug paraphernalia (Selekman, 1989).

I also build rapport with difficult adolescents and their families by using a lot of humor, normalizing and positively relabeling family behaviors, utilizing key client words and belief system material in our therapeutic conversations, and improvising on central family themes. Throughout the first interview, I actively listen for humorous elements in the family's story that I can utilize to make the therapy session more playful. I believe that humor can promote family healing and open up space for new possibilities. By utilizing family members' key words and belief material in our therapeutic questions, we are "staying close" to the family and thus our constructions of their problem situation are more likely to be acceptable to their worldview.

During the therapy session, it is essential for the brief therapist to be able to demonstrate to the adolescent and parents that he or she can provide structure in the session, negotiate goals, and disrupt unhelpful patterns of interaction occurring during the session. This type of therapeutic activity helps give the family confidence in the brief therapist's ability to impact change in their situation. When there is a great deal of arguing and blaming in the therapy room, the brief therapist needs to split up the parents and adolescent and meet with each subgroup separately. This is also a useful strategy when it is not possible to negotiate a mutual treatment goal between the parents and adolescent. The brief therapist can then negotiate separate goals with the parents and adolescent.

ASSESSING CUSTOMERSHIP

De Shazer (1988) has developed a highly practical and useful therapeutic guide for assessing who in the client system is most motivated to work with the therapist in resolving the presenting problem. He has identified the following three different therapist–family relationship patterns: visitors, complainants, and customers. These therapist–family relationship patterns are not fixed, but change as the brief therapist develops *fit* (de Shazer, 1985) and a cooperative working relationship with the family. Following a brief description of each of these therapist–client relationship patterns, I will provide case examples of a visitor and a complainant, and I will offer guidelines for therapeutic task selection.

Visitors

The "visiting" adolescent and her family are usually sent to therapy by some social control agent. Another common scenario in these cases is the youth who is dragged into therapy by concerned and frustrated parents. When asked if there is a problem, the adolescent will typically deny having any difficulties. Most difficult adolescent cases were referred for treatment by a probation officer, a school counselor or vice principal, or a child protective worker. Two useful questions to ask visiting families, which help clarify the referral process and maintain therapeutic maneuverability early on in the first interview, are as follows: "What do you think gave [the referring person] the idea that you needed to go for counseling?"; "What do you think [the referring person] needs to see happen in counseling that would convince [him or her] that you wouldn't have to come here anymore?"

There are three therapeutic strategies that I have found to be useful with visitors. The first intervention strategy involves the brief therapist empathizing with the adolescent, acknowledging the family's dilemma about being coerced into therapy, and accepting whatever goals they may have for themselves. Some of my visiting adolescents have wanted to work on resolving boyfriend/girlfriend problems, learning new ways to change their parents' behavior in relationship to them, or getting the social control agent off of their backs. The brief therapist can set up a split between him- or herself and the social control agent by offering to get the latter off the client's back. This strategy works quite well with court-ordered youth. A final strategy that I may utilize with a more challenging adolescent visitor is the "Columbo" approach. Some youths can make even the most seasoned of brief therapists feel very incompetent. The TV detective Columbo has taught me some valuable lessons on how to be strategic and use my feelings of incompetence with difficult adolescent visitors (see Chapter 4 for more on the "Columbo" approach).

If none of the above strategies have produced a joint therapist–family work project or treatment goal, I simply compliment the clients on whatever they report doing for themselves that has been good for them, such as showing up for our first scheduled appointment, and I do not offer them a therapeutic task. I routinely compliment visiting adolescents for being responsible by coming in and "not blowing the session off!"

The following case example illustrates the utility of setting up a split between myself and the probation officer to help get the latter off my client's back.

Christopher had been referred to me by his probation officer after being caught at school with a "dime" ($10) bag of marijuana in his locker. The incident also prompted a 3-week school suspension. The parents were utterly shocked after finding out about the marijuana incident, for "Christopher had never been in trouble with the law before." Earlier in the first interview, the parents could not identify anything they wanted to see changed or any other problems happening in the family that could have led to Christopher's wanting to use or sell drugs. Christopher denied having a problem with drugs, but admitted that some of his friends abused them. He claimed that he was holding the dime bag for a friend who was being watched at school by the dean. Christopher took a risk in the session with his parents by telling them that he had experimented with marijuana and alcohol in the past. Because the parents were unable to identify any other treatment goal than helping Christopher stay out of further trouble with the law and the school authorities, I spent the majority of the session time eliciting their strengths and resources and discussing their strategies for preventing future legal or school difficulties. Christopher's main goal was for me to get the probation officer off his back. This was discussed during my individual session time with Christopher.

CHRISTOPHER: Mr. Curtis [the probation officer] really pisses me off. He's constantly snooping around my school checking up on me. He thinks I'm a dealer or something. Honestly, I've only smoked weed [marijuana] three times. I actually like beer better, but I do that at parties. Look, I don't have a problem. I don't know why I have to come for counseling. There's nothing wrong with my head.

THERAPIST: It must be a real drag having a probation officer "snooping around" and "checking up" on you at school. How would you like me to get him off your back?

C: Well, that would be great if you could do that, but how?

T: Well, two ways. I know Mr. Curtis well. We have worked together on other cases so he pretty much allows me to call the shots with counseling, you know, how often we meet with your parents. So although we have to meet throughout your nine-month probation period, we will not have to meet weekly. Another way for us to get Mr. Curtis off your back is to prove him wrong, you know, show him that you are not a drug abuser or dealer, by taking responsible steps to turn this situation around. What are some positive steps you will take to prove Mr. Curtis wrong about you at school?

C: Go to all of my classes, stay away from my friends that party ... I don't know, I guess do my homework.

T: What about at home? What responsible steps will you take at home to convince your parents that you're not a drug abuser or dealer?

C: Come home on time on the weekends. Don't drink. Do my chores.

T: When you take all of these responsible steps, what will Mr. Curtis tell you he was most impressed by that you did?

C: Going to my classes. He thinks I've been cutting classes to go party with my friends. Yeah, he will freak when he finds out from my teachers that I'm going to my classes and doing my work.

T: What about at home? Which responsible step will Mr. Curtis be the most surprised with that you will take at home with your parents?

C: Coming home on time on the weekends. He probably thinks that I'm out drinking and partying with my friends all weekend. He doesn't know nothing!

T: Let's prove him wrong together! (We shook hands.)

I ended up having a total of seven sessions with Christopher and his parents over 9 months. Two of these sessions were joint meetings with the parents, the probation officer, and involved school personnel. Christopher had not only successfully terminated his probation, but he took all of the "responsible steps" he had identified in the first interview to "get Mr. Curtis off his back."

Complainants

The complainant can be a parent, a school official, or some other social control agent. Complainants are very concerned about some aspect of the identified adolescent client's behavior, however, they do not include themselves as part of the solution development process. With difficult adolescent cases, a common case scenario involves complaining parents who want the therapist to "fix" their son or daughter through individual therapy. These parents may also complain about not having time in their hectic work schedules to bring their son or daughter in for scheduled therapy sessions.

Because the complainant has tremendous insight into the identified client's behavior, I compliment complainants on their insight into the situation and for being helpful to me in better understanding their concerns. I also compliment them on any other useful coping strategies they report engaging in around the identified client. Two useful therapeutic strategies for the complaining parent are assigning an observation task and having the complainant "think about" the identified client's behavior (de Shazer, 1988).

In the following case, the mother, Lucy, brought her 17-year-old son, Bob, in for therapy because she thought he had a "drinking problem," he was "not doing his homework," and he failed to keep his "bedroom floor clear of dirty clothes and paper scraps." The excerpt below is taken from the first interview, when I met alone with Lucy.

THERAPIST: You have given me a pretty good picture of all of the difficulties and concerns you have with Bob. However, in order for me to have a more complete picture of the home situation, I would like you to pull out your imaginary magnifying glass over the next week and look carefully for all of the times when Bob is not making you worry about him and he is doing the kinds of things you want him to do. Notice what positive steps he will be taking during those times and write those things down.

LUCY: I really do worry too much about him, but I really want to see him stop getting drunk on the weekends with his friends. And his bedroom looks like a pigsty. And his . . .

T: You know, problems are like quicksand, the more we think about them or complain about them, the more we get swallowed up by them. We need to get out of the quicksand and notice what Bob is doing that we want to capitalize on.

L: Maybe you're right; I've been stuck in "quicksand" for a long time and I'm sick of it!

T: So over the next week, I want you to grab your imaginary magnifying glass and notice what's happening with you and Bob when you're not "stuck in quicksand."

Lucy returned the following week with a one-page list of changes she observed in Bob's behavior. He did not "come home drunk on the weekend" and Lucy observed him twice "doing his homework." Lucy also came to the realization that it was "up to Bob to decide to be a pig" with his "messy bedroom" and that this would be "one less worry" for her.

Customers

The customer is the client who presents for therapy wanting to work with the therapist to resolve a specific problem. It has been my clinical experience that customers are typically parents. However, some difficult adolescent clients will decide to become customers when the brief therapist has negotiated a good quid pro quo contract between the youth and her parents. For example, the mother will take her daughter out shopping when she gets up on time to go to school at least two times over the next week. Ideally, having at least one customer in the family sessions is all it takes to resolve the presenting problem. Another useful way to assess the customer in the client system, is to ask the following questions: "Who in your family is most concerned about this problem?"; "Who else?"; [Asking the identified client] "On a scale from one to ten, ten being most concerned about you, what number would you give everybody in your family?"; "What difference will it make to each person in the family when this problem is solved?"

PURPOSEFUL SYSTEMIC INTERVIEWING

The Solution-Oriented therapist asks questions in a purposeful manner, by carefully assessing the family's cooperative response patterns and matching questions with those patterns (de Shazer, 1988, 1991; Lipchik, 1988; Lipchik & de Shazer, 1986; O'Hanlon & Weiner-Davis, 1989). For example, if the use of exception-oriented questions is generating important client exception material, than the therapist should continue utilizing this category of questions and gradually move the family towards the future with presuppositional questions (O'Hanlon & Weiner-Davis, 1989). The purposeful interview is a recursive dance in which the family's verbal and nonverbal feedback guides the therapist with future question category selection. The purposeful systemic interviewing guidelines presented in Figure 3.1. outline the major choice points in selecting or changing question categories in the interviewing process. The various interventive questions discussed in this section can promote self-healing (Tomm, 1987) and liberate families from their oppressive problems by opening up space for new possibilities. I will now present several different categories of questions, offer guidelines for question category selection, and

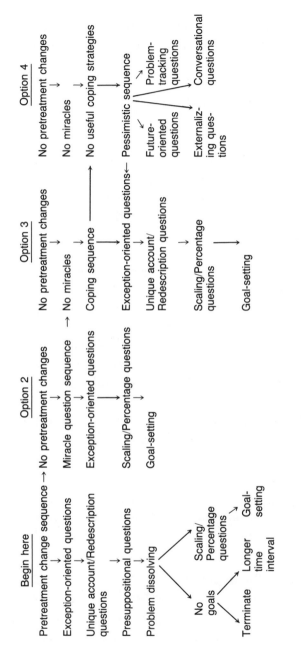

FIGURE 3.1. Guidelines for purposeful systemic interviewing in the first interview.

provide some case illustrations to demonstrate the utility of the various interventive questions in the interviewing process.

Pretreatment Change Sequence

Weiner-Davis et al., 1987, have demonstrated that clients often proactively take steps to resolve their difficulties between the time of the first call to the agency or clinic and the first therapy session. This can frequently be seen with cases on the agency waiting list or where there has been some lag time between the initial call and the first interview. Based on this research and my strong belief that all clients have the strengths and resources to change, I like to begin a first interview in waiting-list or lag-time cases with the question, "So what have you noticed that's better since you first called our clinic?" Not only does this question convey the idea to clients that the therapist believes they have the strengths and resources to change, but it presupposes that changes have already occurred, which can help set in motion the cocreation of a positive self-fulfilling prophecy for them.

The following case example demonstrates the utility of capitalizing on pretreatment changes with a lag-time case (2 weeks after initial call).

Randy, a 16-year-old delinquent boy, had been referred to me for family therapy after having spent 1 month in the juvenile detention center. He was accompanied to the session by his mother, Mary.

THERAPIST: Since Randy got out of the "juvie" [Randy's language], what have you noticed that is better?

MARY: Everything has been great! He's been going to school and following my rules. He's not smoking that marijuana stuff. It's like he's another person.

T: Wow! How did you get him to do all of those "great" things!?

M: Well . . . I told him when I picked him up at the juvenile center that I'm not going to put up with his nonsense anymore and from now on he's going to live by my rules or go to live with his alcoholic father.

After Mary reported some of Randy's changes, I utilized cheerleading and a "how" exception question. The cheerleading helps punctuate exceptions and make them "newsworthy." "How" questions help family members to compliment themselves on their resourcefulness. I spent the remainder of the first interview and subsequent sessions with Randy and his mother amplifying and consolidating the multitude of pretreatment changes. Other pretreatment change questions are as follows: "Is it different for him to do those things!?"; "What will you have to continue to do to get that [exception behavior] to happen more often?"; "How did you do that!?"

"Why Now" Questions

Solution-Oriented therapists believe strongly that the therapeutic context is a place for change and not for "problem talk" (Gingerich et al., 1988). However, it is essential for us to elicit from our clients what specifically led to their pursuing therapy, as a preliminary step toward goal formulation. Therefore, it is helpful to begin an interview with clients who don't report pretreatment changes by asking, "What brings you in now?" or "What would you like to change today?," rather than asking, "What is the problem?" If parents reel off a long list of presenting problems, I ask them, "What would you like to change first?" Once we know what specifically the clients want to work on changing first, a small treatment goal can be negotiated.

Exception-Oriented Questions

With many difficult adolescent cases, it is not so easy early in the first interview to steer away from "problem talk" or negotiate solvable problems and goals. Therefore, the brief therapist needs to actively disrupt the clients' problem-talk interactive pattern and inquire about exceptions (de Shazer, 1988, 1991; Lipchik, 1988; O'Hanlon & Weiner-Davis, 1989). Exceptions take the form of useful patterns of behavior, thoughts, beliefs, and feelings that have helped the client not be pushed around by the presenting problem. These exceptions, when amplifed by the brief therapist, can serve as building blocks for solution construction. Some examples of exception-oriented questions are as follows:

> "You have given me a fairly good picture of the problem you are concerned with, but in order to have a more complete picture about what needs to be done here, I now need to know, when this problem does not happen, what's happening instead?"
> "What are you [the parents] doing differently around Bill [the son]?"
> "How did you come up with that idea!?"
> "Was that different for you to do that?"
> "If Bill were sitting here today, what would he say he would want the two of you [the parents] to continue doing that was helping you get along better?"
> "What will have to happen for that [parental exception] to happen more often?"
> "How will you know when the problem is really solved?"

Rebecca and her mother, Linda, were referred to me by their family physician. Linda was convinced that her 16-year-old daughter had a "depression." Although there were no readily identifiable precipitants nor familial history for depression, after reading a popular magazine article, Linda believed that Rebecca had all of the "symptoms of teenage depression," such as "isolating" from the family, being noncommunicative with Linda, some slight decline in her grades, "being moody," and so forth. Despite the mother's concerns, the family physician did not corroborate her diagnosis, but felt that a little therapy might be useful. Linda brought Rebecca to the first session.

THERAPIST: What brings you in now?

LINDA: Well, I think Rebecca has teenage depression.

T: How do you know that?

L: Well, she has all of the symptoms . . . I think of teenage depression . . .

T: I'm curious, Linda, what's different with Rebecca during the times when she's more up?

L: Well, she's playing her piano, she's helping me out in the kitchen, and I guess she's telling me good things about her boyfriend . . .

T: Did you give her boyfriend the "Good Housekeeping seal of approval," Linda?

L: *(laughing)* He's a good kid.

T: So Rebecca's got good taste in young men?

L: Very good taste.

REBECCA: Yeah, my mom really likes Steven . . . look, I really didn't think we needed to come here. I've been a little bummed about a friend of mine moving away . . .

L: Oh, you mean Helen? I didn't know the two of you were so close?

R: Yeah, after school I used to go over to her house a lot before you came home after work . . .

T: How can your mother be helpful to you at this time in dealing with the Helen situation?

R: Stop asking me twenty questions about being "depressed!" Sometimes my mom gets carried away with magazine articles.

T: Is there anything else she could do or has done in the past with you that has been helpful when you're "bummed?"

R: Talk about it . . . I guess we haven't gone out shopping together in a long time. *(Rebecca looks at her mother, smiling.)*

I saw Linda and Rebecca only one time. Besides utilizing exception-oriented questions, I introduced doubt in Linda's mind about Rebecca's having a "teenage depression" by asking the former "How do you know that?" Rebecca normalized her own behavior by describing it as her being "bummed" about the loss of a friend, which is a temporary and solvable difficulty. I then elicited Rebecca's expertise regarding more productive things her mother could do in relationship to her to help her feel less "bummed."

Unique Account and Redescription Questions

Unique account and redescription questions were developed by Michael White (1988) to assist families in the coauthoring of new stories about themselves and their relationships that counter the dominant stories that have been oppressing them. Unique account questions invite family members to make sense of important exceptions by linking them to particular patterns of interaction or a series of events in time or place (White, 1988b; White & Epston, 1990). Some examples, of unique account questions are as follows: "How did you manage to take this important step to turn things around?"; "What were you telling yourself to get ready for this big step?"

Unique redescription questions invite family members to ascribe significance and new meaning to the exceptions and unique accounts through the redescription of themselves, their family relationships, and significant others (White, 1988b; White & Epston, 1990). These questions empower family members "to operate in the domain of consciousness and to call forth alternative knowledges" (White, 1988b, p. 12). Some examples of unique redescription questions are as follows:

"What does this tell you about yourself that is important to know?"; "How has this new picture of yourself changed how you view yourself as a person?"

The following excerpt is taken from my first interview with Randy and his mother, Mary. I utilize a unique account question with Randy to find out what he told himself in the juvenile detention center that made him decide to turn over a new leaf after getting out.

THERAPIST: What kind of things did you tell yourself in the "juvie" that made you decide, "I'm going to be a different person when I get out?"

RANDY: Well . . . I told myself, "I can do better than ending up in places like this"; "I have to stop smoking reefer"; "I need to stop cutting school"; "I gotta listen to my mom." Things like that, man.

T: Wow! It sounds like you were really doing some heavy soul-searching in the juvie.

MARY: I've really noticed that he's really trying this time.

Throughout the first interview with Randy, I was truly amazed by how much he had changed during his month-long incarceration experience in the "juvie." I frequently made distinctions in the interview between the new responsible Randy versus the old "I don't care" Randy. The mother clearly noticed Randy's growth steps and was a key coauthor in helping her son rewrite his story as a responsible young man pioneering a new direction in life.

Presuppositional Questions

Presuppositional questions (O'Hanlon & Weiner-Davis, 1989) are powerful interventive questions that can be utilized to amplify pretreatment changes and exceptions, to convey the inevitability of change to clients, to elicit the client's outcome goal, and to cocreate a future client reality without problems.

Presuppositional questions can also produce significant changes in client's perceptions and behaviors. Listening carefully to our client's own presuppositions can give us clues as to where they are stuck and what directions to pursue with them. If a family appears to be stuck in the past with their perceptions about their present problem situation, it makes sense to move the therapeutic conversation into the future where there are many more possibilities for change. Some examples of presuppositional questions are as follows:

> "How will you know when you would not have to come here anymore?"
>
> "If you were to show me a videotape of how things will look over the next week when Johnny has stopped breaking curfew, how will the three of you be getting along better?
>
> "What will we see different happening?"
>
> "Johnny, what will we see you doing differently in relationship to your parents?
>
> "If we were to gaze into my imaginary crystal ball after you have 'fixed' [client's language] your relationship with your dad, what kinds of things will we see you and him doing together and how will you be talking to him differently?"
>
> "Suppose we were to run into one another in a month at a 7-Eleven store after we successfully completed counseling together, and you proceeded to tell me the steps you took to get out of counseling, what steps would you tell me you took?"
>
> "Imagine you are driving home from our session today and it had achieved what you were hoping for, what would have changed with your situation?"
>
> "What will a small sign of progress look like in the next week that will indicate to you that you are heading in the right direction?"

Miracle Question Sequence

The miracle question was developed by de Shazer (1988, 1991) to rapidly move clients into a future reality without problems. This question is particularly useful for eliciting from clients their treatment goals and a detailed description of what an ideal outcome picture will look like to them when the problem is solved. I like to move quickly to the miracle question when my clients are negating my exception-oriented questions and are pessimistic about their problem situation. The miracle question sequence is as follows:

> "Suppose the three of you go home tonight and while you are asleep a miracle happens and your problem is solved. How will you be able to tell the next day that a miracle must have happened?"
>
> "What will be different?"
>
> "How will you have done that?"
>
> "What else will be different between the three of you?"
>
> "Who will be the most surprised when you do that?"
>
> "Who next?"
>
> "If I were a fly on your living room wall watching the three of you after the miracle occurs, what kinds of things will I see you doing together?"
>
> "If your sister were sitting here, what would she say that is different about how you and your mother are getting along after the miracle?"
>
> "I'm curious, are any of these miracles happening a little bit already?"

The key to getting the most mileage out of the miracle question is to expand the possibilities, that is, to have family members describe a detailed picture of what all of the miracle-produced changes will look like in every context they interface with and what the significant others in their lives will notice is different about them after the miracle.

The following case example demonstrates the utility of the miracle question for helping cocreate a context for change with a 14-year-old depressed boy and his mother.

Robert had been referred to me by his school counselor for "depression," "school failure," and "poor peer relations." The excerpt below is taken from the first interview after Robert and his mother had negated my exception-oriented questions.

THERAPIST: Suppose the two of you were to go home tonight and while you are asleep, a miracle happened and your problem is solved. How would you be able to tell the next morning that a miracle happened? What will be different?

ROBERT: Well, I would wake up and get out of bed with a smile on my face and tell my dad: "It's time to go to school!"

T: So you will "wake up with a smile" on your face, what else will you be doing differently at school?

R: I will be listening more, paying more attention in class, not asking as many questions, doing my work . . .

T: Which one of your teachers will be most surprised by the new Robert?

R: They will all probably faint!

T: Which one of your teachers will faint first!?

R: I'd probably have to say Mr. Johnson.

T: After you help revive Mr. Johnson, what will be the first thing he will comment to you that has changed about you?

R: "Robert, an A on your Math test!?"

T: Who will be the next teacher to faint?

R: I would have to say Mrs. Williams.

T: After she wakes up, what will her first words be to you?

R: Good job, Robert!

T: What else will be different at school for you?

R: Well, I would have made a couple of friends.

T: Two friends?

R: Yeah. There's this one guy named Juan who I've seen in some of my classes.

T: Will you have approached him or what will you have done with Juan?

R: I will have approached him and asked him if he would like to grab a taco at the El Toro restaurant after school.

T: He strikes you as someone who likes to eat tacos? How can you tell the difference between someone who likes to eat tacos and a non-taco-eater?

R: There's one thing . . . the color of the skin . . . he's Hispanic. *(laughter)*

T: Oh! What about on the home front? If your father were sitting here, what would he say has changed about you after the miracle happened?

I ended up spending close to 30 minutes on the miracle inquiry with Robert and his mother. Besides asking about the changes Robert's father and mother will notice in Robert and in their relationships, I brought into the miracle picture the maternal and paternal grandparents and other relatives. Because Robert and his mother were able to describe in great detail how things would look when the problems were solved, I simply had to prescribe that they engage in the solution behaviors they identified in the miracle picture.

Coping Sequence

With families that tend to be more pessimistic and do not respond well to the miracle question, I shift gears and mirror their pessimistic stance by asking them: "How come things aren't worse?"; "What are you and others doing to keep this situation from getting worse?" Once the parents respond with some specific exceptions, I shift gears again and amplify these problem-solving strategies and ask: "How did you come up with that idea!?"; "How did you do that!?"; "What will you have to continue to do to get that to happen more often?"

In the following case example, I utilized the coping sequence (Berg & Gallagher, 1991) with June, an African-American single parent, who was quite pessimistic about her 16-year-old boy Sid ever changing.

Sid had longstanding problems with underachieving and being truant from school. Early in the first interview, I found myself stuck doing "more of the same" (Watzlawick et al., 1974) by asking exception-oriented questions that were being met with responses from June like: "He's always been an underachiever"; "He's not going to school"; "He's got a bad attitude." When I asked June the miracle question, she could envision neither Sid ever changing nor her being able to do anything differently to impact on his behavior. Sid, on the other hand, was able to spell out numerous miracle behaviors he would be engaging in, two of which he was already doing—completing his homework assignments and going to school! However, June had not made any mention of these big changes on Sid's behalf earlier in the interview.

JUNE: You know, that's the thing I don't like about him . . . he's got a lot of anger inside him . . . I'm not even sure if he went to school yesterday . . . You know, he's your kid and . . .

THERAPIST: I'm curious, how come things aren't worse?

J: Well . . . he's got a good home environment, you know, he's not had to grow up in the slums . . .

T: What else have you been doing to prevent things from getting worse?

J: Well, I make him watch those educational shows on TV . . . we talk a lot, joke and punch . . . he's just rebellious at times.

T: Yeah, teenagers can be real rebellious at times. What else are you doing to prevent things from getting worse? I mean he could be running away, doing drugs, he even came to our therapy session!

J: Yeah, that's a real miracle! I don't know . . . I guess I keep the lines of communication open . . .

T: How do you do that?

J: Well, I make myself available to him and let him know I am concerned and proud of him at times . . . in fact, just the other day, I had complimented him. I had to go to the grocery store and had asked him to not go out until I returned home . . . and he had waited for me!

T: Wow! How did you get him to do that!?

J: Yeah . . . I was so proud of him and he's even gone to school a few days this week . . .

T: Really! So you're already noticing that he's making a little progress? How did you get that to happen!?

J: I guess . . . keeping the lines of communication open, you know, letting him know not to mess around with Mom. When Mom says something, she means it!

T: Yeah, don't "mess around with Mom!"

As readers can clearly see, we made a complete U-turn in the interviewing process. Through mirroring June's pessimism, I was able to move our therapeutic conversation in a positive direction that produced some important parental exceptions. I ended up giving June an observation task to continue to notice all the various things she did in relationship to Sid that further contributed to his turning things around at school and at home.

Scaling Questions

Scaling questions (de Shazer, 1985, 1991) are useful for securing a quantitative measurement of the family problem prior to treatment and presently, and of where they would like to be in 1 week's time. This category of questions is a valuable goal-setting tool and helps maintain a clear focus throughout the course of therapy. Once the family has identified and rated the problem situation on a scale of 1 to 10, the brief therapist's job is to negotiate with the parents and adolescent what each party will have to do to get at least a half to a whole point higher on the scale in 1 week's time. I always like to give my clients the benefit of the doubt when it comes to reporting their higher scores in second and subsequent sessions. For example, if a parent returns to a second session reporting that she had scored a 5 or 6, I give her a 6 minus for the week. Scaling questions can be used to measure a client's confidence level regarding the possibility of resolving their presenting problem. I may ask a parent who has been frequently arguing with her son: "How confident are you on a scale from one to ten, ten being totally confident, that you will resolve this difficulty with your son?" Once the parent provides me with a number on the scale, I can ask her what she will need to do to get a point higher on the scale. This will then become the initial goal for therapy. After utilizing the miracle question (de Shazer, 1988) sequence, scaling questions can be used to negotiate a well-formed treatment goal (de Shazer, 1991) with families (see Figure 3.2). Finally, with more chronic adolescent cases that have had multiple treatment experiences, I may reverse the scale, with 10 being the worst and 1 being the best possible rating of the problem situation.

Marie was referred to family therapy for "running away" and "family problems" by her school guidance counselor. Her mother had been identified as being an "alcoholic" by Marie's counselor. Throughout the first interview, the mother was highly pessimistic and voiced her opinion that "counseling is not helpful" and "has not worked in the past." Once I asked the mother to scale Marie's arguing behavior, the session became more focused and she was less negative. The mother identified two treatment goals for Marie, to stop running away and for her daughter to stop arguing with her all of the time. Surprisingly, I was able to get mother to agree to work on changing the arguing problem first, rather than trying to take on the monolithic goal of stopping the running away behavior.

THERAPIST: On a scale from one to ten, ten being the best, one the pits, how would you have rated Marie's arguing with you four weeks ago?

MOTHER: She was probably at a two, but the shit really hit the fan when she ran away the last time, and now she's grounded.

Family's presenting problems
Smokes marijuana
Never does homework
Never follows parental rules
↓
Miracle question
↓
Family's miracles
Doesn't do drugs
Follows parental rules
Shows more respect
Does homework
Has more freedom
Doesn't yell as much
↓
Scaling questions
↓
Parents presently rate their son at a 3. He will make it to a 4 if he does his homework daily for one week.
↓
Therapist negotiates a more realistic and smaller goal with the parents and adolescent.

Treatment goal
Son does his homework two days
out of five.

Privilege negotiated
Son will be able to come home one hour later Friday night when he achieves the goal established.

FIGURE 3.2. Establishing a well-formed treatment goal.

T: Where would you rate her today?

M: Well, she's been pretty good lately . . . well, I'd have to give her a six.

T: Wow! That's quite a leap for her. How did you get her to move up the scale from a two to a six?

M: Well, I've grounded her and tried not to blow up as much as I used to.

T: What will Marie have to do to make it to a seven?

M: Well, listen to me without putting up a fight. If she could go two days without arguing with me, I would give her a seven.

T: Is there anything you think you could do differently around Marie over the next week that can help make that possible?

M: It's really up to her to change, but I suppose I can try to not blow up as much.

After meeting alone with the mother to further negotiate her treatment goal, I met with Marie before the intersession break to see if she would accept her mother's goal and explore with her if she had a separate goal or any privileges she wanted me to pursue for her with her mother. Marie confidently said she could go for more than 2 days without arguing with her mother.

One week later, Marie and her mother returned with the latter reporting that her daughter had "scored a nine." Marie had gone an "entire week without arguing" once with her mother. I spent the whole second session amplifying all of the family changes.

Percentage Questions

Similar to scaling questions (de Shazer, 1985, 1991), percentage questions help provide a clear focus in treatment and a quantitative measurement of progress in the family's goal area across the course of therapy. Percentage questions also provide the family with a double description (White, 1986) of their problem situation, which can open up space for new possibilities for them. Some examples of percentage questions are as follows: "What percentage of the time does Bill invite you [the parents] to take responsibility for him?"; "What percentage of the time, Bill, do you take responsibility for yourself?"; "What percentage of the time are you standing up to bulimia versus bulimia's getting the best of you?"

The following case example illustrates how percentage questions can be utilized to cocreate a double description (White, 1986) of a parent's pathological label of her daughter's behavior, with each of the therapist's descriptions indicating more normal and solvable adolescent behaviors.

Marjorie sought therapy for help dealing with her daughter's "behavior-disordered" problem. Sarah, Marjorie's 16-year-old daughter, had been chronically "violating" the "rules," "constantly argu-ing" with Marjorie, and sometimes "ditching school." The excerpt below is taken from the first interview.

THERAPIST: What brings you in now?

MARJORIE: My daughter Sarah is "behavior disordered." She never listens to me, we're constantly arguing, she's always violating my rules, and there are days where I'm convinced she is ditching school . . . and . . .

T: How do you know she is "behavior disordered?"

M: Well . . . that's what her school counselor thinks . . . what do you think?

T: I'm curious, what percentage of Sarah's behavior would you consider to be normal teenage rebelliousness versus obnoxious-ness?

M: Well . . . I . . . I never thought of it that way . . . but if I had to give you percentages . . . I would say she's probably sixty percent rebellious and forty percent obnoxious.

T: Help me out, how were the percentages different four weeks ago?

M: Well four weeks ago, I would have given her a much higher ranking on the rebelliousness end of things.

T: What percentage number would you have given her back then?

M: Oh, I would have to say . . . she was really infuriating me back then . . . I would have given her ninety percent on the rebellious-ness end of things!

T: Wow! How did you get her down to sixty percent of the time only being rebellious? What have you been doing differently?

M: Well I'm not yelling as much. I have been going for walks.

T: What else have you been doing to help her be less rebellious?

I ended up spending the remainder of the session eliciting other important exceptions on Marjorie's behalf that had not only helped her better cope with Sarah's normal teenage behaviors, but that also helped her have a more cooperative relationship with her daughter. After three sessions of therapy with Marjorie, she was totally convinced that Sarah was a "normal teenager." Sarah's final percentages ended up being "fifty percent rebellious" and "fifty percent obnoxious" in our termination session.

Pessimistic Sequence

If a family continues to be pessimistic about the problem situation after I have utilized the coping sequence with them, I will shift gears and match their unique cooperative response pattern by utilizing the pessimistic sequence (Berg & Gallagher, 1991). Despite the therapist's best efforts to create hope and a context for change, highly pessimistic parents will insist that their adolescents' behaviors will continue to get worse and produce dire consequences. Therefore, it makes the most sense to join these parents on their own level. Often this line of questioning will enable family members to generate some useful problem-solving and coping strategies to better manage their difficult situation. Some examples of pessimistic questions are as follows: "What do you think will happen if things don't get better?"; "And then what?"; "Who will suffer the most?"; "Who will feel the worst?"; "What do you suppose is the smallest thing you could do that might make a slight difference?"; "And what could other family members do?"; "How could you get that to happen a little bit now?" The pessimistic sequence may also help parents remember past successful parenting strategies that they can utilize with the present crisis situation.

Externalizing Questions

Externalizing the problem (White, 1984, 1985, 1986, 1987, 1988a, 1988b; White & Epston, 1990) is a useful therapeutic option with highly entrenched families that are not responding well to Solution-Oriented questions in the interviewing process. The family's presenting problem can be externalized into a problem lifestyle, career, pattern, or objectified oppressive tyrant. When externalizing the family's presenting problem, it is most important to carefully utilize family members' language and belief material about the problem. Otherwise, family members will interpret your new construction of their problem situation as being "too unusual" and will disregard it (Andersen, 1991). According to Michael White (White & Epston, 1990), externalizing the problem can therapeutically accomplish the following six things with entrenched families:

1. Decrease unproductive conflict between persons, including those disputes over who is responsible for the problem;
2. Undermine the sense of failure that has developed for many persons in response to the continuing existence of the problem despite their attempts to resolve it;
3. Pave the way for persons to cooperate with each other; to unite in a struggle against the problem and to escape its influence in their lives and relationships;
4. Open up new possibilities for persons to take action to retrieve their lives and relationships from the problem and its influence;
5. Free persons to take a lighter, more effective and less stressed approach to "deadly serious" problems;
6. Present options for dialogue, rather than monologue, about the problem. (pp. 39–40)

The following case example illustrates the therapeutic utility of externalizing the problem in disrupting a longstanding blame–counterblame pattern of interaction in the family.

The Browns were a remarried family. Both Fred and Lisa had been married once before. Their previous marriages were reportedly quite stormy, and Sean, Lisa's only child from her first marriage, was being identified as the current family problem. Sean had longstanding problems with stealing, being disruptive in school, and not responding to Lisa's limits. Sean greatly disliked Fred and did not get along with the latter's two sons from his first marriage. Throughout the first interview, there was a great deal of blaming and arguing across family subgroups. My attempts to elicit exception material and utilize the miracle question were thwarted.

However, both parents pointed out how "blaming" had riddled their previous marriages and was clearly a problem in the present family drama. I decided to capitalize on this oppressive past "blaming" pattern by externalizing it and moving the focus off of Sean as the problem.

THERAPIST: How long has this "blaming" pattern been pushing all of you around for?

FRED: Well, I was married to my first wife for five years and Lisa and I have been together for the past two years.

LISA: I have been dealing with this blaming thing for about nine years and Sean's father and even Sean still blames me for everything now.

SEAN: Can I leave now? I'm sick of her [his mother] bullshit! She's always jumping on my case all of the time!

T: Do you see how blaming got in between the two of you right there and made you lock horns with one another?

F: You know he's right. We need to stop dumping on one another and close the door on our pasts. This is our new family and we have to make it work.

T: I'm curious, Lisa, have you noticed any times lately where this blaming thing was trying to make you "dump" on Sean, but you stood up to it and did something else?

L: In fact, yesterday I was tempted to "dump" on Sean about how he reminds me of his father when he leaves his things laying all over the house, but I asked him nicely to put his dirty clothes in the laundry basket.

S: Yeah, usually you're screaming at me about what a "pig" I am . . .

T: Sean, I think I'm going to give your mom a high five for achieving that victory over blaming. (*Gave Lisa a high five and, much to my surprise, Sean gave his mother one as well.*)

The remainder of the interview was more positive and we focused our attention on the various things family members were doing to both accept invitations from the blaming pattern to "dump" on one another as well as discussing important things they were already doing to stand up to it. I gave them a task to keep track on a daily basis of the various things they did to achieve victories over the blaming pattern. They were also asked to keep track of blaming's victories over them. I recommended that they train as a family for their big battle with blaming because "it will not die easily, for patterns are powerful things." Sean was placed in charge of developing a family exercise program because he was the "true athlete" in the family. Fred and Lisa were in charge of charting their daily victories and losses with blaming.

Future-Oriented Questions

For our clients, the future is fertile ground for change because it has not happened yet. We can be coarchitects with our clients in designing the kind of future realities they wish to have. Research indicates that those individuals who can envision a future of mastery and success at performing tasks will tend to outperform those subjects that anticipate hypothetical failure (Sherman, Skov, Hervitz, & Stock, 1981). Spanos and Radtke (1981) and Spanos (1990) have found in their hypnosis research that having subjects absorb themselves in imagining future events has a powerful hallucinatory effect. The subjects actually believed that their imaginings were a reality for them. These studies help provide some empirical support for the use of imagination and the imagined future in the therapeutic arena.

Future-oriented questions are particularly useful with "past-bound" (Tomm, 1987), chronic, and entrenched family cases. According to Penn (1985), future-oriented questions "promote the rehearsal of new solutions, suggest alternative actions, foster learning, discard ideas of redetermination, and address the system's specific change model" (p. 299). Some examples of future-oriented questions are as follows:

"When Johnny gets a job, who will be the most surprised in the family?"

75

"Who next?"; "If we were to gaze into my imaginary crystal ball after you got over your 'anger and bitterness' [client's words] toward your father, what will we observe happening that is different about your relationship?"

"What else will be different?"

"When I'm gazing into the crystal ball, what will I notice that is different about you that will surprise me the most?"

"If you were to show me a videotape of your family after we successfully completed counseling together, what kinds of changes will we observe on the video?

"What else will be different?"

Problem-Tracking Sequence

Once the brief therapist has exhausted the possibilities with the Solution-Oriented model, one good therapeutic option is to shift gears into more of a MRI Brief Problem-Focused (Fisch et al., 1982; Watzlawick et al., 1974) therapeutic approach. The focus of therapy then becomes not only attempting to alter the family's perception of their problem situation, but also actively disrupting the problem-maintaining sequences of interaction in the family. Problem-tracking questions (Palazzoli, Boscolo, Cecchin, & Prata, 1980) can elicit from family members a detailed videotaped description of the circular patterns of interaction around the presenting problem. After securing this information, the brief therapist will then have several focal points at which to disrupt the circular problem-maintaining patterns (see Chapter 6 for pattern intervention strategies). Some examples of problem-tracking questions are as follows: "If you were to show me a videotape of how things look when your brother comes home drunk, who confronts him first [asking a sibling of the identified client], your mother or your father?"; "After your mother confronts him, what does your brother do?"; "How does your mother respond?"; "Then what happens?"; "What happens after that?" Ideally, the brief therapist will secure a detailed picture from family members regarding the specific family patterns that have maintained the presenting problem. Pattern intervention (O'Hanlon, 1987) can then be utilized to disrupt the problem-maintaining patterns.

Conversational Questions

Narrative family therapy approaches (Andersen, 1991; Anderson & Goolishian, 1988a; Deissler, 1989; Lussardi & Miller, 1991) are gaining in popularity in the family therapy field today. The Narrative approach is particularly useful with some highly entrenched and traumatized families that have had multiple treatment experiences. I have also found this approach useful with cases where there appear to be family secrets and multiple helpers from larger systems involved. It has been my clinical experience that using only the Solution-Oriented Brief Therapy approach may disempower these families by editing the long stories they need to tell about their problem-saturated situations. Solution-Oriented questions can shut down the therapeutic conversation by blocking family members from feeling free to tell their unique stories about their family drama. Conversational questions (Anderson & Goolishian, 1988a; Anderson & Goolishian, 1988b) are the Narrative therapist's primary tool for helping keep the therapeutic conversation going. These questions are opened-ended and are informed from a position of "not knowing" as opposed to "preknowing." By asking questions from a position of "not knowing," we place ourselves in the position of learning (Anderson & Goolishian, 1988a). When family members feel free to retell their stories, this can lead to the disclosure of the "not yet said" (Anderson & Goolishian, 1988b) and the generation of new meaning and possibilities for the family. Some examples of conversational questions are as follows:

"You have seen many therapists, what do you suppose they overlooked or missed with you?" "If I were to work with another family just like you, what advice would you give me to help that family out?"

"Who had the idea in the family to go for therapy?"

"If there were one question you were hoping I would ask, what would that be?"

"If there was one issue in this family that has not been talked about yet, what would that be?"

"Who in the family will have the most difficult time talking about this issue?"

The following case example illustrates the importance of therapeutic flexibility in the interviewing process.

I had begun my first interview with Sharon and her mother utilizing Solution-Oriented questions. Sharon, 16 years old, had been brought to me for her chronic headache problem. After many years of extensive testing, the family physician and other headache specialists had not been able to find any physical signs for this problem. Sharon had been plagued by headaches since she was 12 years old. Solution-Oriented questioning had failed to generate exceptions. At this point in the interview, I decided to abandon this type of questioning and asked conversational questions instead. The excerpt below is taken from the first interview.

THERAPIST: Who in your family gives you the biggest headache?

SHARON: My dad. He is so bigoted and conservative. He's always putting down gays, Jews . . .

MOTHER: Yeah, he can be like that at times, but he's getting better.

Throughout the interview, Sharon appeared to get quite emotional when she talked about her father. I decided to meet alone with Sharon to give her more room to tell her story, particularly about her relationship with her father.

THERAPIST: If there were one issue in your family that has not been talked about yet, what would that be?

SHARON: *(begins to shake and cry)* Well . . . um . . . well *(crying and shaking)* I think I'm gay . . . and I'm so afraid if my dad finds out he'll never talk to me again. Please don't tell my mom *(crying and shaking)*.

T: I won't say a word until you are ready to talk about it. How long have you thought you were gay?

S: Since around sixth grade.

T: This has been a heavy load you have been carrying around in your head hasn't it?

S: I'll say. The safest place for me to write down my thoughts about it is in my creative writing class assignments. I play all of the different characters in the stories. Sometimes I'm a man or a half boy and half girl.

Sharon and I continued to talk about her lifestyle choice in future sessions. Much to my surprise, in the second therapy session Sharon disclosed to her mother that she was gay. Initially, her mother was quite shocked, but after three family sessions she came around to accepting it. This was a "newsworthy" experience for the mother in that it helped explain why Sharon was having her stress-related headaches and reacting so strongly to her father when he would criticize gays. The mother also successfully got Sharon's father to be a little more understanding with Sharon.

Consolidating Questions

Consolidating questions are useful for amplifying pretreatment changes and for reinforcing family changes that occur in second and subsequent sessions. At times, I may use my imaginary crystal ball (de Shazer, 1985) and videotape metaphor (O'Han-lon & Weiner-Davis, 1989) to invite clients to provide a visual description of how things will have further improved with their situation 2 weeks to 6 months down the road. Some examples of consolidating questions are as follows:

"What will you have to continue to do to keep these changes happening?"

"How did you get that to happen?"

"What would you have to do to go backwards?"

"What would you have to do to prevent a major back-slide?"

"How will you get back on track again?"

"If I were to invite you to my next parenting group to serve as guest speakers, what helpful advice and pointers would you give those parents?"

"Let's say this was our last counseling session together, what fun things will you be doing during this time?"

"If we were to gaze into my imaginary crystal ball three weeks down the road, what further changes will we see happening?"

When conducting the purposeful systemic interview, the brief therapist needs to carefully read the family's nonverbal and verbal feedback, as well as be prepared, at any given moment in the session, to shift from one question category to another. By "staying close" to the family, we are making room for the familiar and opening up space for new possibilities.

MECHANICS OF THE SOLUTION-ORIENTED BRIEF FAMILY THERAPY INTERVIEW

After establishing good rapport with each family member, I begin the interview by exploring what the trigger was that led the family to pursue therapy now, as well as inquire about pretreatment changes. As early as possible in the initial interview, I engage family members in change talk (Gingerich et al., 1988) and attempt to move them into the future with presuppositional questions (O'Hanlon & Weiner-Davis, 1989). Sometimes having the family speak only about present and future changes can dissolve the idea that they have a problem. I have experienced this with clients who present with significant pretreatment changes. If the parents identify a problem area they wish to see changed with their adolescent, I attempt to deconstruct the problem into a more solvable behavior and negotiate a smaller and more realistic treatment goal with the family. The miracle question (de Shazer, 1988) and scaling (de Shazer, 1985) or percentage questions are useful tools during the goal-setting process. However, if no goal can be negotiated between the parents and adolescent, the interactions in the therapy room are destructive, and the miracle question (de Shazer, 1988) fails to produce exceptions and a treatment goal, I separate the family and meet with subsystems.

BRAINSTORMING WITH THE PARENTS

When meeting alone with the parents, I use the time to explore with them their past and present attempted solutions and negotiate a separate treatment goal with them. While exploring with the parents their attempted solutions, I ask the following questions: "Has there been anything that you have tried in the past with your son that worked with some other problem that we may want to use now?"; "Has there been something that you thought about trying out with your daughter, but for whatever reason you didn't think it would work?" This type of question capitalizes on the parents' resourcefulness and creativity, as well as helping to generate potential solutions. I punctuate the parents' resourcefulness and creativity through cheerleading, which helps make these potential solutions "newsworthy" to them. When I establish a separate treatment goal with the parents, it usually involves having them experiment with new behaviors they wish to pursue around their adolescent—for example, to go 2 out of 7 days without yelling at their son. At times, the parents cannot readily identify a treatment goal, but want to do something about the son or daughter's problematic behavior. If they request a homework assignment, I may offer them an observation task (Molnar & de

Shazer, 1987) or the "do something different" task (de Shazer, 1985), depending on their unique cooperative response pattern.

EMPOWERING THE ADOLESCENT

I like to utilize individual session time with adolescents to accomplish the following: increase rapport, establish a separate treatment goal, negotiate the parent's treatment goal, make room for them to tell their stories about their family situations, and find out if there are any privileges they wish me to advocate for them with their parents. Because the majority of difficult adolescent clients are "visitors" (de Shazer, 1988), I accept whatever goals they identify for themselves, which may be completely unrelated to what brought them in for therapy. However, it has been my clinical experience that if the therapist joins well enough with the adolescent, the youth may be willing to do whatever the parents and the therapist request, particularly if a privilege could be earned as a reward. With adolescent cases, the brief therapist needs to be an intergenerational negotiator. Most adolescent clients tend to cooperate with therapists that pay attention to what *their* goals and expectations are, not just what the parents want. I like to ask my adolescent clients, "How can I be helpful to you?" This conversational question can open the door for the adolescent to identify his or her goals and expectations, share what privileges he or she wants, and tell his or her story about the family drama. In Chapter 4, I will discuss six effective engagement strategies for difficult adolescents.

WORKING WITH A REFLECTING TEAM

Approximately 40 minutes into the hour, I have the reflecting treatment team (Andersen, 1987, 1991; Lussardi & Miller, 1991), who have been observing the session from behind the one-way mirror, come into the therapy room, while the family and myself go behind the mirror to listen to their reflections about the interview. One at a time, the reflecting team members reflect on significant family themes of resourcefulness and family strength, compliment the family on important exceptions, offer new constructions of the family's problem situation, and reflect on the interviewing therapist's ability to cooperate with and assist the family in the change effort. According to Lussardi and Miller (1991), "it is the movement from one explanation to many, which allows information, new meanings, and the possibility for new behavior to occur" (p. 235). When giving reflections, team members should begin with qualifiers such as "I'm astonished by . . ."; "I'm impressed by . . ."; "It seems to me . . ."; "I'm struck by . . ."; "Could it be . . ."; or "I wonder if . . ." It is very important that the team members are careful not to bombard the family with too many ideas. The reflecting team members also need to "stay close" to the family by carefully utilizing the family members' language and belief system material in their reflections.

Another useful reflecting team format is to have two therapists in the therapy room: one therapist in the observing position and the other therapist interviewing the family. At the intersession break, the therapists will reflect in front of the family. This will be followed by the family's reflections on the therapists' conversation. This reflecting team format can be used with families that have requested having the team member present in the therapy room.

I have observed that families listening to the team's reflections behind the one-way mirror appear to be very absorbed in the reflecting team's conversation about them, and even in a trance. In fact, I frequently have observed head nods (yes-set hypnotic responses), parents smiling or shedding tears, and nonverbal gestures of affection exchanged between family members. Often the treatment team's reflections make family exceptions even more "newsworthy" to the family, alter family members' outmoded beliefs about their situation, and open up space for the "not yet said" (Anderson & Goolishian, 1988b) to be disclosed by a family member. Once the reflecting team's conversation is over, we switch rooms again and the family and the interviewing therapist reflect on the team's reflections.

Because the reflecting team has such an empowering effect on the family, it is not always necessary for the therapist and team to offer the family a therapeutic task. After we discuss the reflecting team's conversation, if it appears that the team's reflections were not "newsworthy" to the family and there is still a strong concern on the family's behalf about a specific problem they want to actively do something about, I ask them if they would like a homework assignment. At this point, I have the team come into the room and brainstorm with them one or two therapeutic tasks that fit with the family's unique cooperative response pattern. The team and I then present to the family the tasks we have selected or designed, and we give them a choice regarding the tasks they would like to do for homework. With some first interviews, however, the team and I can only come up with one particular task that fits best with the family's unique cooperative response pattern, and we recommend it as being useful to them at the time.

When I am working solo, I still take a break and "meet with myself" to think about the family's story, to construct compliments, and design or select an appropriate therapeutic task for the family. Prior to taking my intersession break, I ask the family if they would like a homework assignment or not. After my minibreak I share my compliments, offer some new constructions of the family's story, and present a useful therapeutic task for them to experiment with. With some families, if they do not request a therapeutic task or if they present themselves as visitors, I only offer my reflections. I call this portion of the session "the editorial." At the conclusion of my editorial, I schedule another appointment with the family.

GUIDELINES FOR THERAPEUTIC TASK DESIGN, SELECTION, AND IMPLEMENTATION IN THE FIRST INTERVIEW

In this section of the chapter, I will present useful guidelines for designing, selecting, and implementing therapeutic tasks in first interviews. As a rule of thumb, all compliments, alternative constructions of the family's story, and therapeutic tasks evolve out of the interviewing process. The designed and selected therapeutic task must fit with the family's unique cooperative response pattern. De Shazer and his colleagues at the Brief Family Center in Milwaukee, Wisconsin, have developed a highly useful and accurate system called BRIEFER (de Shazer, 1988; Gingerich & de Shazer, 1991), which can aid brief therapists and trainees with clinically deciding which task(s) to select for a particular case situation. I have found the BRIEFER II (Gingerich & de Shazer, 1991) flowchart to be quite useful when working with difficult adolescents and their families. I will now present the BRIEFER II guidelines for intervention selection and provide case examples to demonstrate the utility of the task selected.

FORMULA FIRST SESSION TASK

If a family presents with a vague complaint, BRIEFER II recommends the "formula first session task" (de Shazer, 1985, 1988; Gingerich & de Shazer, 1991). Because this is a vague task, it will fit with the family's unique cooperative response pattern. De Shazer (1985) contends that this task is likely to work with this type of clients because "the prophecy is that something worthwhile is going to be noticed between the first and second sessions, and the likelihood is that, indeed, that will be the case" (p. 139).

As mentioned earlier, with visitor families who cannot identify a goal or joint work project, BRIEFER II recommends giving compliments only and no therapeutic task (de Shazer, 1988; Gingerich & de Shazer, 1991). Visitors will not do tasks because they are not customers for therapy, at least during the first interview.

PRETEND THE MIRACLE HAPPENED

If the family is unable to identify any exceptions, BRIEFER II suggests that the brief therapist give the "pretend the miracle happened" task. The following case example illustrates the effectiveness of this task with a chronic acting-out adolescent and his family.

Paul was referred to me for his "attention deficit disorder" problem, and for chronically violating his parents' rules, "stealing money" from his parents, and hitting his teacher. My first session with Paul was right after he had been discharged from a local psychiatric hospital. Paul had been admitted to the hospital after striking his school teacher. In the earlier part of the interview, I attempted to elicit exceptions from the parents, but they negated my exception-oriented questions. After asking the miracle question (de Shazer, 1988), I was able to secure two important changes that the parents would notice with Paul: "Paul would not be swearing at us" and "He would not fight us when we say 'No!'" Paul reeled off a long list of changes that he envisioned occurring with himself and family members after the miracle happened. I decided to separate the family when the parents became negative again after the miracle inquiry. I met alone with Paul and asked him to pick 2 days to pretend to engage in his parent's miracle behaviors so we could "blow their minds!" Paul thought this was a "real neat" idea, particularly the idea of watching how his parents would react differently to him when he was pretending. One week later, the parents came back stating that "a miracle must have happened!" They reported at least eight significant exceptions on Paul's behalf. Most importantly "Paul did not swear" or "fight" with his parents once over the entire week. Future family sessions involved prescribing more of what works. Therapy was successfully completed by the fourth session.

DO SOMETHING DIFFERENT

With case situations where the parent's goal is not related to the reported exceptions, BRIEFER II recommends the "do something different" task (de Shazer, 1985; Gingerich & de Shazer, 1991). This "skeleton key" intervention is particularly useful with overinvolved or highly reactive parents. I explain to parents that their son or daughter has got their number, he or she knows every move that they are going to make. After this short rationale for their need to be less predictable, the parents are given the following directive, "Between now and the next time we meet, I would like each of you to do something different, no matter how strange, weird, or off-the-wall what you do might seems" (de Shazer, 1985, p. 123). The following case example shows how a parent's off-the-wall behavior can impact change in her son's longstanding behavioral difficulties.

Deborah and her 17-year-old son, Seth, were referred to me because the latter had been placed on probation for shoplifting, assault and battery charges, gang involvement, and school truancy. According to Deborah, Seth "ran the household" through "breaking things" when angry and "winning power struggles" with her. The more she would "yell at Seth" and attempt to place limits on him, the more he would act up. Deborah was at her wits' end and was ready to try anything with Seth. Because Seth boycotted our initial therapy session, I had to intervene through his mother. I gave Deborah the "do something different" task. One week later, Deborah came back reporting dramatic changes in Seth's behavior. What Deborah had decided to do was that whenever Seth would push her buttons, she would sing the children's song "Row, Row, Row Your Boat." This totally disarmed Seth and led to comments like: "Are you okay?"; "What's wrong with you?"; "Maybe you need to see the therapist more often." Apparently, the more Deborah engaged in her off-the-wall behavior, the more Seth's behavior changed. Seth became more respectful towards his mother and stayed out of further legal difficulties. The biggest surprise for me was having Seth show up to our third therapy session wanting to help his "freaked-out mother."

PREDICTION TASK

BRIEFER II recommends the prediction task (de Shazer, 1988; Gingerich & de Shazer, 1991) for cases in which the reported exceptions occur spontaneously and are not deliberate. The prediction task can set in motion a positive self-fulfilling prophecy for the clients. In the following case example, both the parents and their "bulimic" 16-year-old daughter, Patricia, could not explain why at least 3 days per week the latter would not "binge and purge."

Patricia and her parents had been referred to me through an HMO. Patricia had been diagnosed as having bulimia nervosa by a psychiatrist she had seen for a year. Because "nothing had changed" with "Patricia's bulimia problem," the parents decided to pursue family therapy. Early in the first interview, I discovered that there was a randomness to the occurrence of binging and purging episodes. However, neither the parents nor Patricia could identify the reasons for why the exceptions were happening. I decided to give the family the prediction task. The night before the next day the parents and Patricia were separately to predict whether the latter would be "standing up to bulimia and not allowing it to push her around," and, in the middle of the next day, to try to determine what she did to be victorious. The next week, Patricia came in with her parents happily reporting that "six days out of seven" they had "achieved victories" over bulimia. Both the parents and Patricia reported several exceptions that had contributed to the family's victories over bulimia. Since the prediction task had worked so well, I continued to use it in future sessions.

MORE OF WHAT WORKS

Finally, if the family readily reports engaging in deliberate exception behaviors, BRIEFER II suggests that the brief therapist should "prescribe more of what works." Observation tasks (de Shazer, 1988; Molnar & de Shazer, 1987) are particularly useful with these families to amplify their present exception patterns of behavior and to have them keep track of further changes they make.

If the family does not request a therapeutic task or they are visitors, I will keep things simple, follow the BRIEFER II guidelines for therapeutic task selection, and not recommend a homework assignment. However, some difficult adolescents and their families do not respond very well to the basic Solution-Oriented Brief Therapy approach alone and will perhaps require more storytelling time, a pattern interruption intervention (O'Hanlon, 1987), or a more complex therapeutic strategy as per Michael White (White & Epston, 1990). I will discuss these strategies further in Chapter 6.

CONCLUSION

The first interview is the beginning and the end of treatment. The brief therapist's skill in building rapport, interviewing for change, and accurately selecting the most appropriate therapeutic task in the initial session will significantly determine the outcome picture the clients will have.

F O U R

EFFECTIVE STRATEGIES
FOR ENGAGING
DIFFICULT ADOLESCENTS

E ngaging the difficult adolescent can be an arduous task for even the most skilled therapists. Frequently, these youths have been labeled "resistant," "uncooperative," "anti-authority," and "unmotivated" by the referring person and other helpers. With many of these cases, past therapists have attempted "more of the same" solutions (Watzlawick et al., 1974) with these youths, for instance, "putting the parents in charge" of the adolescent without attending to the adolescent's needs in relationship to the parents. Oftentimes, past therapists have done the majority of their intervening through the parents and have not joined well enough with the adolescent, or have failed to secure from the adolescent what he or she would like to get out of therapy. It is my contention that it is possible to generate changes on the parental and adolescent levels simultaneously. In this chapter, I will present six engagement strategies that capitalize on the strengths and resources of the adolescent and help foster a cooperative therapeutic relationship. Case examples will be provided to illustrate the utility of these engagement strategies with difficult adolescents.

HUMOR AND SURPRISE

The therapist's use of humor has been empirically proven to be an effective tool for engaging difficult adolescents (Alexander,

Barton, Schiavo, & Parsons, 1976; Newfield, Kuehl, Joanning, & Quinn, 1991; Parsons & Alexander, 1973; Selekman, 1989a, 1989b). Adolescents have reported liking therapists that have a good sense of humor, are playful, and create a lively therapeutic climate. With every new adolescent case, I listen carefully for the humorous twists in the family's story that I can utilize in the joining process and the therapeutic task design. I also like to capitalize on the humorous bodily posturing of the adolescent to further enhance the engagement process. For example, I have conducted some family sessions slouched ridiculously low in my chair to mirror the adolescent's nonverbal behavior, which typically prompts smiles and laughter from the family and the youth. I purposefully self-disclose humorous events from my own adolescence to normalize the adolescent client's present struggles with a particular developmental task. Finally, I may share a humorous joke that offers the adolescent and parents a new way of looking at their situation and can lighten up the atmosphere in the therapy room.

The following case example demonstrates how the therapist's use of an appropriate joke that, in some ways, mirrors the family's story can generate new possibilities in the family's perception of their situation.

The parents had brought Jim in for therapy because of his "antisocial attitude" and abuse of alcohol and marijuana. According to the parents, Jim would "blast his terrible music for hours" after school. They felt his heavy metal music was "fueling his antisocial attitude" and substance abuse. For 1 year, the parents had been having major power struggles with Jim over his heavy metal music and substance abuse. The excerpt below is from the first family session. Because the atmosphere was tense, I decided to take a risk and share a humorous heavy metal music joke I had heard.

THERAPIST: I was recently at a comedy club downtown and heard a heavy metal music joke that I would like to share with all of you that I believe you will get a kick out of. I'm sure all of you have heard about all of the controversy on TV regarding the subliminal messages that heavy metal records are supposed to give to teenagers like: "Jump off the bridge"; "Shoot your dog"; et cetera. Well, imagine this scene . . . the teenagers are rushing home from school and playing their heavy metal records backwards and the subliminal message is: "Cut the grass!" "Cut the grass!" And all of the teenagers are mowing their lawns! The parents are freaking out and fainting . . .

FATHER: *(laughing)* That's funny!

MOTHER: *(laughing)* I would probably faint!

JIM: *(with a smile on his face)* That would really trip them out if I mowed the grass . . . I hate cutting the grass. *(turns toward his mother)* You would really faint if I cut the grass?

M: You haven't cut the grass since you were ten years old . . .

F: I would probably faint because you rarely do anything around the house.

T: *(turning to Jim)* It sounds like your parents don't think you can do it, but I agree with you that it would really "trip them out" if you cut the grass. Which one of your parents will be the first to faint?

J: Probably Dad would.

F: Thanks, son, but you're probably right. I am more sensitive to big surprises than Margaret [mother] is.

T: When your dad faints after you have cut the grass, will you dump a bucket of water over his head to revive him?

J: That would be funny. . . . *(laughing)* No . . . I think I would wait to see how tripped out he will look when he sees the great job I did on the lawn.

After discussing in great detail the parents' reactions to Jim mowing the lawn, the atmosphere in the therapy room had lightened up and the family interactions had greatly changed. The parents and Jim mutually agreed that his mowing the lawn would be a good initial treatment goal. In 1 week's time, not only did Jim mow the lawn, but he kept the volume level of his stereo down, and the parents reported no signs of substance abuse. As a reward for his great week, the parents took Jim to one of his favorite Italian restaurants and bought him some headphones so he could "blast his music as loud as he wanted to into his own ears."

In therapy sessions with adolescents, I try as much as possible to keep the sessions upbeat and make room for improvisational surprises. One of my former cases provides a good example of how my therapy sessions take the form of an improvisational theater production.

William, a 15-year-old, "depressed" high school freshman, was referred to me for "fleeting thoughts of suicide," "poor social skills," and "failing grades." William and his mother came to the session very concerned about his problems. After asking the miracle question (de Shazer, 1988), I successfully generated a number of useful exceptions and cocreated a context for change with the family. One important exception was that William attended a martial arts class. To further empower William and challenge the dominant story (White & Epston, 1990) that he was "depressed," I had him give the team (behind the one-way mirror) and I a live demonstration of his best judo and karate moves. Following William's great performance, the team came into the room from behind the one-way mirror and together we gave him a standing ovation. After the team left the room, I commented to the mother how she "must feel safe with William around." I also asked William if I could feel his biceps. When complimenting William at the end of the session, I shared with him that the team and I would like to take martial arts lessons with him. This compliment produced a big smile on William's face. Over four sessions of therapy, William successfully improved his grades, made two friends at school, and no longer displayed any signs of being depressed.

UTILIZATION

The engagement strategy of *utilization* was developed by Erickson (de Shazer, 1985; Erickson & Rossi, 1983; Erickson, Rossi, & Rossi, 1976; Gordon & Meyers-Anderson, 1981; O'Hanlon, 1987). While establishing rapport with his clients, Erickson would listen carefully for specific strengths and resources he could utilize in their presenting problem areas. Erickson believed that therapists should enable their clients to do what they do best, by capitalizing on their strengths and resources (Gordon & Meyers-Anderson, 1981). The following case example illustrates the therapeutic usefulness of the utilization strategy with a challenging adolescent case.

Ramon, a 16-year-old Latino male, was brought for therapy by his mother, Juanita, for his aggressive and violent behaviors at school and at home. For 3 years, Ramon had been getting into fights at school, arguing with teachers, punching holes in his bedroom wall, and threatening to strike his mother. Ramon had been in individual therapy twice before, but none of his behaviors had changed. Juanita had been "divorced from Ramon's father for five years." She attributed Ramon's aggressive and violent behaviors to his father's past physically abusive behavior. Apparently, the father used to beat Juanita in front of Ramon and disciplined Ramon harshly with a belt. Ramon had not had any contact with his father since the parental divorce.

Early in the first interview, I discovered that Ramon was a very talented artist. In fact, I had the luxury of seeing some of his best drawings in his sketch book that he brought to the session. Ramon loved to draw Marvel Comics' super-heroes like the "Hulk," "Fantastic Four," "Thor," and so forth. However, over the past year, Ramon had been utilizing most of his artistic talents drawing evil-looking "super-villains" that would "kill the good guys" and "take over the universe." While admiring Ramon's drawings, I noticed that he took pride and joy in his work and liked the fact that I was taking an interest in his artistic abilities. Ramon also shared with me that some of his most creative moments in coming up with new "super villains" occurred "after a fight" with his girlfriend or his mother, or after a "bad day at school." After hearing this important exception material, I began to think about how I could utilize Ramon's artistic abilities and constructive coping strategy in the problem area.

Before meeting alone with Ramon, I spent session time with Juanita to explore exceptions and past helpful attempted solutions. Juanita could neither identify any exceptions nor envision future miracles with Ramon's behavior. Prior to our first family session, Juanita had called the police on Ramon for threatening her.

Ramon had begun to blame his mother for his aggressive behavior by claiming that she "yells at" him "too much." Juanita agreed that there had been times where the more she would overreact to Ramon, the more he would escalate his aggressive behavior and so forth. While meeting with Juanita, I explored with her whether she would like a homework assignment that could assist me in helping her son. Juanita decided to experiment with the observation task (Molnar & de Shazer, 1987) that I wanted to give her, which would focus her attention on exception patterns in Ramon's behavior.

During my individual session time with Ramon, I decided to capitalize on his artistic abilities, particularly at drawing evil-looking "super-villains." I asked Ramon if he would be willing to do an experiment that would be fun and that would "blow his mother's mind." I also pointed out that another benefit of doing the experiment would be having his mother "yell at" him less. Ramon agreed to try my experiment. I gave him the following instructions:

"Whenever you are mad about anything or at anybody [bad day at school, girlfriend, mom], I want you to zoom up to your bedroom and draw some of the most evil-looking 'super-villains' your creative mind can come up with. I want you to keep drawing until you are no longer mad. I will be looking forward to seeing all of your new 'super-villain' characters in your sketch book next week."

I concluded the family session with compliments for Juanita and Ramon. One week later, Juanita came in reporting a big reduction in Ramon's temper outbursts and threatening behaviors. She had not received "one call from the school." Juanita was most surprised by Ramon's "not fighting back" with her. Ramon reported that his mother was "yelling less" and that they "hardly got into it" over the week. The biggest surprise for me was hearing that Ramon had decided to extend his experimental behavior to the school context as well. Ramon proudly showed me his new "super-villain" entries in his sketch book. Future sessions consisted of prescribing more of what was working, consolidating gains, and collaborating with concerned school personnel.

WORKING THE OTHER SIDE OF THE FENCE

In my clinical practice with difficult adolescents and their families, I have found it to be quite advantageous to provide the adolescent with individual session time. Research indicates that both the adolescent and his or her parents expect therapists to do this (Newfield et al., 1991; Selekman, 1989a, 1989b). The individual session time can be used to further join with the adolescent, negotiate the parents' goals, establish a separate goal, and elicit from adolescents the privileges they would like to get from their parents. The majority of difficult adolescent clients I have worked with have been quite surprised when I asked them, "How can I be helpful to you?" In their previous therapy experiences, their parents' wishes for how they "should act" or what they "had to change" took precedence. They were never asked questions such as: "What would you like me to change with your parents?"; "Is there a privilege you would like me to go to bat with your parents for you?" This type of open-ended question can provide the therapist with invaluable information that can be utilized in negotiating a quid pro quo contract with the adolescent's parents. By working the other (adolescent's) side of the fence, the therapist can greatly strengthen his or her therapeutic alliance with the adolescent and be an effective intergenerational negotiator for the family.

In the following case, I will present an excerpt from my first family session with Julie.

Julie had been on probation for the past 3 years for shoplifting, possession of marijuana, and truancy. She had received multiple therapy experiences since age 11. Now at age 16, the parents were seriously contemplating shipping her off to boarding school. During the first half of our session, I was able to secure the parent's treatment goal for Julie, which was that she get up on her own accord in the morning in time to catch the school bus at least twice over the next school week. The excerpt below is from my individual session time with Julie.

THERAPIST: You know, I have heard a lot from your parents about what they want to see you change, but what I would really like to know from you is, how can I be helpful to you?

JULIE: Well, they are always bitching at me about every little thing. I need some new clothes and they tell me "Tough!" Even when I do things right like go to school or come home on time they never notice.

T: That's got to be frustrating. So if there was one thing you would like me to change with your parents what would that be?

J: Well, if you can get them to stop bitching at me so much . . .

T: During one week's time, how many days out of seven do they usually "bitch" at you?

J: Seven days!

T: Now, since they have been bitching at you for such a long time and so frequently, how many days out of seven would be realistic for them in terms of making a small amount of progress? How many days out of seven could they cut back on the bitching that would be a good start for them?

J: If they could go at least one day without bitching at me I would be happy.

T: When they are not bitching at you, what will they be doing instead?

J: Maybe saying something nice to me for once like: "Good job!"; "I can tell you are trying." See, I never hear these kind of things anymore.

T: So in the past, they used to praise you?

J: Yeah . . . before I got on probation.

T: What were you doing differently back then that made them want to praise you?

J: Well . . . I was doing better in school, I didn't party . . . you know, smoke weed . . . those kind of things.

T: Back then, how did your parents praise you and what other kinds of things were they doing differently that you liked?

J: Well, they told me that they were proud of my good report cards,

Mom took me out to buy clothes, my dad used to joke around with me more . . .

T: We are running out of time, but I want to thank you for letting me know about what you want for you and how together we can work on changing your parents' "bitching." Their goal for you, which sounded pretty easy, was for you to set your alarm clock and get up on time to catch the school bus at least twice over the next week. My hunch is, if you really wanted to blow your parents' minds you would do this at least a few times over the next week.

J: No problem! If I really wanted to, I could get up on time for the bus and stay in school at least three times over the next week.

After complimenting the family, I gave an observation task that consisted of each family member keeping track of what each member does that they wanted to continue to have happen. The family came back 1 week later more hopeful, positive, and reporting a number of exceptions. Julie had had 5 days of getting up on time to catch the school bus. She noticed that her parents were "bitching" at her "less" and actually "praised" her at the end of the school week. Besides amplifying all of the family changes, I successfully negotiated with the mother and Julie a time for them to go shopping together.

When utilizing this engagement strategy, it is important that the therapist join well with the parents and demonstrate his or her commitment to helping them achieve their goals with their adolescents. By carefully working *both* sides of the fence, the therapist will be in a better position to negotiate realistic goals, expectations, and privileges.

ADOLESCENT AS EXPERT CONSULTANT

Difficult adolescents who have had multiple therapy experiences have a wealth of knowledge about what therapists should and should not do with them and their parents. I may ask the adolescent, individually or with the family, the following questions: "You have seen many therapists before me, what do you suppose they missed with you?"; "What should a new therapist do with you that will make a difference?"; "If I were to work with a teenager just like you, what advice would you give me to help her (him) out?" These open-ended questions invite the adolescent to tell the story of past therapy experiences, convey the idea that therapy with me is collaborative, and can foster a cooperative working relationship.

Barbara, a 16-year-old bulimic, had been in three inpatient psychiatric eating disorder programs and had had five outpatient treatment experiences with psychologists and psychiatrists. The parents brought Barbara to see me after her discharge from an inpatient psychiatric 3-month eating disorder program. According to the parents, Barbara had "relapsed" shortly after getting out of the hospital. She was "binging and purging again." While meeting with the whole family, I asked the miracle question (de Shazer, 1988), which created hope for the parents and helped them more clearly articulate what they needed to do differently around Barbara. Barbara, on the other hand, had very little to say regarding what her "miracles" would look like. After meeting briefly with the parents to explore their attempted solutions and treatment goals, I spent some individual session time with Barbara to better connect with her and explore what she would like to get out of therapy.

THERAPIST: I thought it could be helpful if you and I had a little bit of individual space time together without your parents around. They really talk up a storm!

BARBARA: You're not kidding! That's part of the problem . . . they always do this in counseling . . .

T: Talk up a storm?

B: Yeah . . . all of the counselors let them talk too much, you know, like my mom goes off on a long speech on all of the new books she has read on bulimia and anorexia and how she saw so and so on the Oprah show the other day . . . this is why I usually don't say too much in counseling . . .

T: So past counselors have allowed your parents to talk too much in your family sessions. What other things have your past counselors or doctors done with you that you didn't think were helpful or turned you off?

B: Well . . . some of the doctors I saw in the hospital were always trying to get inside my head. I hate that! Tell me how you feel? You know, stupid shit like that. I had this one psychologist put words in my mouth and said that I "binge and purge to get even" with my "parents because they go away on vacation" a lot. That's a crock of shit! Basically, a lot of my friends do this throwing up thing to lose weight so we can get into those tight skirts.

T: Barbara, can you think of any other things I should do differently with you and your parents that former counselors failed to do?

B: Yeah, with my parents . . . don't let them talk so much about what they have read or saw on TV, they begin to sound like all those other counselors. I know my parents love me, but try and get my mom to stop worrying so much about me. Everyday I hear: "Are you okay, honey?"; "Should I not buy potato chips and cookies at the store today?"; "Can I help you with your homework?" This drives me crazy!

T: Which one of those things would you like to see changed first with your parents, the long monologues or getting your parents to worry about you less?

B: The last one. I get real nervous when they worry about me a lot. That's when I really pig out and purge, when I'm real nervous.

T: Any other things that your parents do that make you feel like pigging out and purging?

B: When they try and pick my friends for me. Like they tell me to stay away from two of my closest friends because they had similar problems.

As the reader can clearly see, placing Barbara in the expert position opened the door for her to tell her story about why past treatment experiences did not help her. I learned what I needed to do differently with Barbara and her parents. The added bonus was discovering the specific parental behaviors that inadvertently maintained the bulimia problem. Through the use of pattern intervention (O'Hanlon, 1987) and having Barbara keep track of what she did to overcome the urge to (de Shazer, 1985) "pig out," we were able to resolve the bulimia problem.

THERAPIST'S USE OF SELF

The purposive use of self-disclosure has been shown to be a useful therapeutic tool with difficult adolescents (Selekman, 1989a, 1989b; Newfield et al., 1991). It is crucial that the therapist's self-disclosed material fits with the adolescent client's presenting dilemma. Adolescents have reported that they like counselors that "had been there," in terms of experiencing similar struggles as a youth. However, not all therapists have experienced stormy adolescent periods in their lives, nor are familiar with street lingo. These therapists can use themselves in other ways, such as using humor, telling stories, and sharing their gut reactions or absurd ideas in the interviewing process with the adolescent.

The case example of Steve, a 17-year-old substance abuser, demonstrates how purposive use of self-disclosure can normalize the adolescent's present struggles and also offer the young person some new ideas for problem solving. Although Steve had a long history of treatment for delinquent acting-out behavior, he and his mother were currently at an impasse over his spending too much of his free time with his girlfriend. The other hot issue for the family was Steve's refusal to cut his long hair in order to get a job. The excerpt below is taken from the first family interview with Steve during my individual session time with him.

THERAPIST: So your mom has been on your case a lot lately about your girlfriend, cutting your hair, and getting a job?

STEVE: Yeah, I'm sick of her damn harping! She's always ragging at me about everything. I've got a few possible jobs lined up. I ain't going to cut my hair for nobody! I went to this one picture framing store . . .

T: You know, when I was your age, I was a bad dude too. I had a long maxi army coat, high-top black leather boots, a big 'fro out to here (*physically showing him how round and high my afro was*). My parents wanted me to get a job too. I also said "I ain't going to cut my hair" to get a job. But you know what, I got turned down left and right by employers because I looked like a wild man from Borneo!

S: (*laughing*) You're wild!

T: Once I trimmed that 'fro down, I finally nailed a job. Then, I had money to take my girlfriend out instead of bumming off my parents all of the time.

S: Maybe you're right, because I'm kind of sick of bumming money from my mom and lately she hasn't given me nothing. Karen [Steve's girlfriend] has had to pay for us lately which is kind of a drag for me.

T: The bottom line is that no employer is going to hire a young person that looks like a wild man, you know, like a stoner [drug abuser]. The other thing about getting a job is that you'll have money to buy yourself things that you like, you know, tapes and clothes.

S: That sounds casual, okay, dude. The next time you see me hopefully I'll have a job, but I will cut my hair.

Because I joined well with Steve earlier in the family session, I decided to make use of self-disclosure to normalize his struggles regarding not wanting to cut his hair and shared with him my own solution to this dilemma as a youth. My self-disclosed material was acceptable to Steve's belief system because it mirrored his own situation. Two weeks later, Steve came to the second session sporting a stylish-looking haircut and happily reporting that he had landed a job working in a video store.

THE "COLUMBO" APPROACH

Some difficult adolescent clients make us feel highly in-competent as therapists. Often, these tough adolescents are court-ordered to therapy or have a long history of involvement with mental health professionals. The popular TV police detective, Columbo, has taught me some valuable skills for engaging some of the toughest adolescent clients. Columbo has no trouble allowing his clumsy and incompetent style to show with potential suspects. He convincingly empathizes with the suspect's loss of the murder victim and the uncomfortable situation. While joining with a potential suspect, Columbo uses compliments to butter him or her up. Throughout the entire investigation process, Columbo asks questions from a position of "not knowing" (Anderson & Goolishian, 1988b, 1991b) and presents himself as being confused about who committed the murder and how it occurred. This keeps the murder suspect off balance and eventually leads him or her to help Columbo solve the crime through leading him to important clues or incriminating themselves in some way.

David, an African-American 16-year-old, was court-ordered for 1 year of family therapy for stealing car radios, home burglary, and suspected gang involvement. In the first session, David was accompanied by his mother and his 12-year-old brother, George. Ever since David had been arrested for stealing car radios and home burglary, he denied engaging in any of these behaviors. The mother reported that she thought that David was probably "running with a gang." This was her biggest concern at intake. David had already been in therapy five times for his acting-out behavior. Two of these times, he had refused to go for further sessions after the initial interviews. During the majority of our first session, David had very little to say about why he had to go for counseling or what he saw as the problem. The excerpt below is taken from my individual session time alone with David.

THERAPIST: It must be a real drag for you to have to go for counseling again (*fidgeting with my pad of paper*). Whoops! (*dropping my pad of paper*)

DAVID: What's wrong with you, man! Are you nervous or something?

T: Well . . . a little. I'm surprised that my supervisor gave me your case. I mean your situation is way over my head. I don't get it. The judge ordered you to go for counseling. For what? I mean you say that nothing happened and the police got the wrong guy. I'm really confused *(looking puzzled)*.

D: Well . . . well, I didn't break into that man's crib [house], that was some other brothers that did that. I grabbed me a few car radios in the hood [neighborhood], but I don't do the other things.

T: *(playing dumb)* "Crib?" "Hood?" What do you mean? Maybe I'm old-fashioned or something.

D: You don't know nothing, man! Crib means house. A hood is where you live, you know.

T: Oh . . . now I see. You mean neighborhood. Help me out . . . oh by the way, thanks for the help with the new language you taught me. Anyways, help me out . . . did the judge or the probation officer tell you what they wanted you to accomplish in counseling?

D: Well . . . I think he said I got to stay away from the Lords [street gang] and not get busted anymore.

T: Did they mention anything about what you're supposed to do at your "crib?"

D: You're a trip man! *(laughing)* You're something else, man. Follow the rules. Go to school, you know.

The Columbo approach proved to be quite effective for helping me get in the door with David. My bungling therapist style made it difficult for David to feel threatened by me. I also made it clear to him that I was neither a social control agent nor an extension of the court system.

Future therapy sessions focused on helping David steer away from the street gang lifestyle, assisting the mother with some new parenting skills, and collaborating with the probation officer. Because boxing was one of David's strengths, I hooked him up with an adult friend of mine who coached talented Golden Gloves boxers.

CONCLUSION

In this chapter, I have presented six useful engagement strategies for difficult adolescent clients. With the majority of my difficult adolescent cases, I have found it helpful to utilize a combination of these engagement strategies in first family interviews. The various engagement strategies selected for any one particular case are based on the unique cooperative response pattern of the adolescent, the family's goals, and on what I need to do differently as a therapist in relationship to the adolescent that can help generate a therapeutic change. Brief therapists will find these engagement strategies to be quite effective in rapidly fostering cooperative working relationships with adolescents.

F I V E

ORGANIZING A SOCIAL ECOLOGY: COLLABORATING WITH HELPERS FROM LARGER SYSTEMS

L ong before Second Order Cybernetics (von Foerster, 1981; von Glasersfeld, 1984; Kenney & Ross, 1983; Maruyama, 1974) thinking became the new epistemological framework for family theorists, Auerswald (1968, 1972) had stressed the importance of therapists' adopting an ecological perspective, that is, focusing on the interactions between clients, their families, helpers from larger systems, and the community. Auerswald's (1968, 1972) pioneering theoretical ideas provided the groundwork for later prominent family theorists to expand on his ecological perspective. The Milan Associates (Boscolo et al., 1987) developed the idea of the "significant system," that is, they believe it is necessary for the therapist to intervene with all those individuals involved in trying to solve the client's problem, as well as considering the impact of the therapist's own interventions on the other members of the "significant system." Coppersmith (1985) refers to the significant system as being a "meaningful system." Goolishian and his colleagues have described the significant system as being a "problem-organizing, problem dissolving system" (Anderson & Goolishian, 1988b). Bogdan (1984) contends that problems are an "ecology of ideas."

The Milan Associates were heavily influenced by theoretical ideas from the fields of cognitive biology (Maturana & Varela, 1988) and radical constructivist theorists (von Foerster, 1981; von Glasersfeld, 1984), particularly the latter group's notion of "observing systems," rather than "observed systems"

(Boscolo et al., 1987). For the Milan Associates, the therapist needs to include him- or herself as part of the observation of the client system being treated. When other helpers are involved with a therapist's case, these helping professionals are considered part of the problem system and community of observers that have coalesced around an identified problem. The client system is no longer being viewed as a separate, observed entity requiring major repair work by a privileged therapist who knows what is "best" for the client.

Independent of the Milan Associates, family therapy teams worldwide have developed their own unique systemic approaches for working with the family–multiple helper problem system. At the Houston–Galveston Family Institute, Goolishian and his colleagues (Anderson & Goolishian, 1988b, 1991a, 1991b, Anderson et al., 1986; Goolishian & Anderson, 1981) have developed a highly respectful therapeutic approach for working with chronic and difficult family cases in which multiple helpers are involved. In Europe, the Milan Associates and the innovative work of Goolishian and Anderson have been highly influential on treatment teams in Ireland, Norway, and Germany. The Dublin group has applied these theorists' ideas to the challenging therapeutic context of working with incest victims, their families, and the network of helpers involved with these cases (McCarthy & Byrne, 1988; Kearney, Byrne, & McCarthy, 1989). Andersen and his colleagues in Tromso, Norway have developed an innovative Reflecting Team consultation approach for treating difficult and stuck cases (Andersen, 1987, 1991). Deissler (1989, 1992), in Marburg, Germany, has done some pioneering work with psychiatric clients, their families, inpatient treatment teams, and the larger mental health delivery system.

In this chapter, I will present an ecosystemic approach for working with the family–multiple helper problem system, offer practical suggestions for how to cultivate cooperative and collaborative relationships with helpers from larger systems, discuss the role of the therapist, and provide some case examples.

107

CULTIVATING COOPERATIVE
AND COLLABORATIVE RELATIONSHIPS

The difficult adolescent client often has had frequent encounters with representatives from the juvenile justice system and local police departments, with school personnel, mental health and drug rehabilitation programs in the community, and some involvement with child protective workers. In any one community, a therapist will typically find that the communications are poor among these larger systems, the coordination of services is disjointed, and splitting is a common dynamic that occurs between the larger systems' representatives and the family. Because of the above-mentioned difficulties, I have found it useful to go out into the community and proactively develop close working relationships with helpers from larger systems and attempt to create bridges between my clinic and the representatives from the various helping systems. I have also found it useful in my clinical work to collaborate with clergy, community leaders, and adolescent clients' peers.

Over the years, I have worked with a number of youths that have been involved with the police and the juvenile justice system. Besides making the time to go out and visit local police departments to familiarize myself with the youth officers and meet police social workers, I have found it useful to schedule occasional lunch dates with these key individuals. I try to schedule monthly lunch dates and office meetings with probation officers as well. I like to use these lunch meetings to build rapport and to find out ways we can cooperate better on cases. I am very interested in learning from helpers what I need to do differently as a therapist and co-collaborator, and what I should continue to do with them and our mutual cases together. With some court-involved adolescent cases, my good rapport with judges helped make a difference with treatment outcomes. It is essential for therapists to find out from judges their views regarding treatment for youth and their expectations of therapists.

When interfacing with school personnel, I have found it useful to conduct meetings over lunch to address communication problems and generate new ways to cooperate better. Not only is it important to develop good working relationships with the administrative staff and school social workers, but it is helpful to secure the guidance department and teaching staff's input with cases and treatment expectations as well.

With representatives from psychiatric and drug rehabilitation programs, I like to become familiar with their treatment philosophies and program components, as well as secure information from the treatment teams about what their follow-up aftercare expectations are with cases being referred to me. Many of the agencies and hospital-based programs that have referred cases to me, welcome family transition sessions prior to the youth's discharge from the program. If aftercare groups and other services are being provided to my clients, I extend invitations to involved program therapists to participate in our family therapy sessions or family–multiple helper meetings.

ROLE OF THE THERAPIST

Once I have conducted a macrosystemic assessment with the adolescent and the family to determine the individuals that comprise the problem system, I will have the family sign release of information forms so I can freely converse and collaborate with these key individuals during our family–multiple helper meetings and when providing advocacy for clients in the community. Organizing family–multiple helper meetings is tedious work, particularly trying to coordinate everyone's schedules for joint meetings. Whenever possible, I will try to engage as many as possible of the key members of the problem system that the family wanted to be present in our meetings together. Sometimes, however, this proves to be a futile task with some helpers because of their oppressive caseloads or schedules. In these situations, I will have my clients prepare a one-page summary of the highlights of the family–multiple helper meeting and mail copies to the absent helpers. I will also set aside some time in my schedule to try and arrange separate meetings at the absent helpers' various offices. Unless this outreach work is done by the therapist, the absent helpers will be stuck viewing the client's problem situation in one particular way and engaging in the same attempted solutions, which can contribute to the maintenance of the problem system. We need to maximize the opportunities for the concerned helpers involved with our adolescent cases to notice changes and hear the cases be communicated about differently (Anderson et al., 1986) by significant others in the adolescents' social ecologies.

The first and foremost responsibility of the therapist in the context of the family–multiple helper meeting, is to cocreate a dialogical conversational space that makes room for both the familiar and for new possibilities. This process can only evolve through the therapist's use of "multipartiality" (Anderson & Goolishian, 1988b)—that is, the therapist sides simultaneously with the client's and helpers' varied views of the problem situation. She accomplishes this through being nonjudgmental, conversing in the client's and helpers' language, and offering his or her therapeutic opinions as tentative ideas, rather than as the ultimate truth. The therapist is a respectful listener, a cocollaborator, and is prepared at any point in the therapeutic conversation to change his or her opinions or ideas. The therapist asks questions from a position of "not-knowing" (Anderson & Goolishian, 1988a, 1991b). Buddhist students were taught by their ancient Masters the value of "Don't Know Mind," which is forever fresh, open, and fertile with possibilities (Mitchell, 1988). Lao-tzu (Mitchell, 1988) taught his students the following wisdom, "Wise men don't need to prove their point; men who need to prove their point aren't wise. The Master doesn't seek fulfillment. Not seeking, not expecting she is present, and can welcome all things" (p. 15).

Harlene Anderson, the director of the Houston–Galveston Institute who co-pioneered the therapeutic tool of "not-knowing" with Harry Goolishian, had the following to say about this respectful therapeutic position (Anderson & Goolishian, 1991b):

> By not-knowing we mean a general attitude and belief that the therapist does not have access to privileged information, that the therapist can never fully understand another person, and that the therapist always has a need to know more about what has been said or what has not been said. Not-knowing means having humility about what you think you know. Not-knowing means that understanding is always on the way. Not-knowing means being informed by the client.

Change occurs in the family–multiple helper therapeutic context when new narrative meanings about the client's problem situation are generated, which in turn can lead to problem resolution and the dismantling of the problem system (Anderson & Goolishian, 1988b, 1991a).

CASE EXAMPLES

SUICIDAL OR DÉJÀ VU?

Laura, a 16-year-old high-school junior, was referred to me by her school social worker for what was described as a "severe depression." The school social worker shared with me in our initial telephone conversation that Laura had been "looking very depressed" for the "past month." Her academic performance had "dramatically declined" due to her "failure to complete homework assignments." Laura's English teacher was also quite "worried about" the former's "depressed state." The English teacher had reported to the school social worker that she had observed Laura "sitting in the far corner of the room with her head down" on several occasions. The assistant dean of the high school had also been made aware of Laura's "depressed condition" by the school social worker and agreed that she was a "high-risk" student requiring immediate therapeutic intervention. Over the past month, Laura had had two counseling sessions per week with the school social worker.

In my first interview with Laura and her mother, I explored with them their understanding about how they had gotten referred to me for family therapy. The mother shared with me that the school social worker was "overreacting" and "too intrusive" with Laura. She further added that Laura was "having a hard time adjusting" to her recent "relationship break-up with John." They had been "going steady" for 2 years. Laura agreed with her mother's interpretation of her situation and voiced her upset feelings about being "shadowed" by the school social worker. Laura openly admitted that she was "very bummed out" about John's breaking up with her, but that she would not take her life because of it. According to Laura, the school social worker had asked her in every one of their counseling sessions together if she had "suicidal thoughts." The mother reported that she had called the assistant dean numerous times to complain about the school social worker's "over-involvement" with her daughter and had "requested that she not see her anymore for counseling."

In this initial session, besides exploring what Laura and her mother were doing to better cope with the former's "relationship break-up," I conducted a macrosystemic assessment with the family to determine with them who the key members of the problem system were. We mutually agreed that the problem system consisted of myself, the school social worker, the English teacher, the assistant dean, Laura, and her mother. We also decided that it would be most advantageous to combine individual family therapy sessions with joint family–school meetings. To close out our first family session, I had Laura and her mother sign written release of information forms that would allow me to discuss their case situation with the school members of the problem system.

Present at the first family–school meeting at the high school were the school social worker, the English teacher, the assistant dean, Laura, her mother, and myself. Because the school social worker had referred Laura's case to me, I began the meeting by inviting her to share her story about the identified client and the events leading to the referral. I also asked her, if she could rewrite her original story about Laura, what would a good outcome be? For the school social worker, a good outcome Laura story would be "a young lady not depressed and back on track with her academics." I asked similar questions of each of the meeting participants and had them reflect on each others' comments. Laura's mother shared her concerns that the school had "greatly overreacted" to her daughter situation and that Laura was "not suicidal!" The mother's ideal outcome story for Laura was that Laura would be "completely over the loss of John" and that the school would be "off Laura's back." Laura shared with the group that she was already "taking steps" to get over breaking up with John and was "catching up" with her school assignments. Her ideal outcome story was that she would begin to date again and she would no longer be "shadowed" by the school social worker.

At this point in the meeting, the school social worker began to cry and self-disclose the "not yet said" (Anderson & Goolishian, 1988b) of her personal story about how her "sixteen-year-old daughter had committed suicide." This was the first time the assistant dean, the English teacher, Laura, her mother, and I had ever heard this. Once the school social worker began to disclose her painful story, I noticed a dramatic shift in both Laura and her mother's defensive position toward the school personnel, particularly the school social worker. Spontaneously, Laura and her mother offered their deepest sympathies to the school social worker. The assistant dean and the English teacher were also highly supportive. By the end of the meeting, we all mutually agreed that I would continue family therapy sessions to further help Laura get over the loss of her boyfriend, John, the school social worker would discontinue her counseling sessions with Laura, and that we would have another family–school meeting 1 month later to assess further case progress.

During the month-long interval, I conducted two more family therapy sessions to further amplify Laura's effective coping strategies in putting the loss of John behind her. By the second family therapy session, Laura had not only "caught up" with her "school work," but she had met a "cute guy" on the football team. In our second family–school meeting, everyone, from the school social worker to the mother, reported observing considerable changes in Laura's behavior. We decided as a group that we would discontinue the family–school meetings because of Laura's progress and that I would offer the family one more check-up session 3 months later.

ESCAPING FROM THE GANG LIFESTYLE

Anna and her son, Pedro, 14 years old, had been referred for family therapy by his probation officer for car radio theft, assault and battery charges, chronic curfew violation, and gang involvement. Anna was born in Mexico and, since she had moved to the United States, she had experienced both emotional and financial hardship. Her ex-husband, Ramon, was an alcoholic, was physically abusive, and had had many affairs while they were married. As much as she wanted to go to college to pursue a professional career, Anna had to surrender this dream because of her child-care responsibilities and stressful waitressing job. Anna had four children from her relationship with Ramon. The sibship consisted of three boys, Pedro being the oldest sibling, and Isabella, who was 5 years of age. Anna's only support system in the community was her priest and two Latino girlfriends.

Pedro boycotted my first family therapy session. Anna reported in the initial family session that she was most concerned about Pedro's gang involvement and his coming in after midnight on the weekends and some weekday nights. I explored with Anna her attempted solutions in trying to resolve Pedro's problematic behaviors and elicited from her the key members of the problem system. Anna reeled off a long list of family friends and helping professionals. The family–multiple helper problem system consisted of the following individuals: myself, a local police officer, the probation officer, the school social worker, two of Anna's girlfriends, the priest, a child protective worker, the school principal, and the leader of the community crisis team. I invited Anna to tell me if she thought it would be helpful to bring some of these important people together to assist us in resolving Pedro's difficulties. Anna thought that joint meetings with all of these key individuals would be a great way of working together. I had her sign release of information forms and pointed out that we would need Pedro's signature and cooperation with this method of working as well. Anna made it clear to me that she would make sure that Pedro came to our next family session.

One week later, Pedro came to our session, but maintained a defensive posture throughout most of the interview. When I met with Pedro alone, he became less defensive and liked the idea that the family–multiple helper meetings would ultimately "help get some of these adults off of his back" once they notice the progress he "will be making while we are working together." We also talked about how the local police department had him "pegged as a gang banger" and how "they will be closely monitoring every move" he makes "on the streets." After our brief conversation, Pedro readily signed several release of information forms. Finally, I asked Pedro if there were any other key individuals he would like to include in our family–multiple helper meetings. Pedro was in agreement with his mother's list of the individuals who should be included in meetings.

After 2 weeks of playing telephone tag with the key members of the problem system, I finally was able to schedule our first family–multiple helper meeting. The following individuals came to the meeting: the school social worker, the probation officer, the child protective worker, a concerned local police officer, the priest, the team leader of the community crisis team, Anna, and Pedro. Prior to this meeting, Pedro's father had died from a heart attack and Pedro had been suspended from school after getting caught with a bottle of Jack Daniels whiskey in the boys' restroom. The whiskey incident had occurred after Pedro found out about his father's death.

I began the meeting by briefly joining with each provider. Because the probation officer had referred Pedro to me, I started the meeting by having him tell the story of how he decided to refer the case to my clinic. Besides sharing with the group all of the reasons why Pedro had been placed on probation, he also pointed out that he thought "Anna could greatly benefit from learning some parenting skills." His outcome goal for Pedro was for the latter to stay out of further legal difficulties by getting out of his Latino street gang. At this point in the meeting, the school social worker brought up Pedro's whiskey-related school suspension and said she was "concerned about how poorly" the client was "coping with the loss of his father."

Suddenly, Anna took the floor and shared her story about her past relationship with Ramon (Pedro's father) and why they had divorced. All members of the family–multiple helper meeting, including Pedro, had their eyes fixed on Anna and were listening intently to her story. Anna shared with the group that Ramon was "very loving with Pedro" when he was a toddler, but that Ramon began to "distance from the family" when he started "abusing alcohol and marijuana." Pedro and the rest of the group got a chuckle out of hearing about the time that Ramon gave Pedro a sip of his beer and he rushed into the bathroom to spit it out. Pedro asked his mother, "Did I really do that?"

Following this amusing chapter in Anna's story about

Ramon, Pedro heard for the first time all of the reasons why his mother had divorced his father. This included Ramon's physical and emotional abuse of Anna, as well as the multiple extramarital affairs he had had before Pedro reached his adolescence. After hearing this painful material, Pedro began to shed a few tears and put his arm around his mother for support. This was the first time I had observed Pedro showing affection toward his mother.

Prior to ending this highly productive meeting, the probation officer shared with Pedro that he would not bring him before the judge for the possession-of-alcohol incident. Pedro gave a big sigh of relief and smiled. I brought to the group's attention that Pedro had resolved his curfew violation problem and had not gotten in any further legal difficulties. We all gave Pedro a big round of applause for the behavioral progress he had been making. Another change in Pedro's behavior was that he had stopped beating up on his 13-year-old brother, Fernando. The last time Pedro had beaten up his brother, the child protective services were called in to intervene. The family priest shared with Pedro that he would explore with his colleagues if there was some work that he could do around the church. We all agreed to meet as a group in 4 weeks.

Subsequent family–multiple helper meetings served to further empower Anna and Pedro. The priest found some odd jobs for Pedro to do around the church to help keep him off the streets. Anna had saved up some of her money and I helped her secure some scholarship funds from a local community college to take a few classes. Pedro continued to make progress in all areas of his life and successfully terminated his probation. There was a total of six family–multiple helper meetings over a 6-month period. Meetings were conducted every 4 weeks.

WITH A LITTLE HELP FROM MY FRIENDS

Adolescent clients' peers can be an invaluable resource for brief therapists to utilize when co-constructing solutions with families and when stuck in therapy (Selekman, 1991a). With some of my stuck cases, I will utilize an adolescent client's peers as an expert consultation team to help offer us some fresh ideas. The following case illustrates the power and creative ingenuity of peer-generated solutions with stuck adolescent cases. Liz, 16 years old, was referred to me by her probation officer for possession of marijuana, substance abuse, chronic violation of parental rules, and school truancy. Liz had participated in Narcotics Anonymous (NA) meetings in the past and found them "boring and unhelpful" for relapse prevention. She also had been in a 28-day inpatient chemical dependency program. Two weeks after being discharged from this program, Liz returned to marijuana use.

After two sessions of brief therapy, the parents and I had collaboratively disrupted the problem-maintaining pattern of superresponsible parental behavior around Liz, which in the past had led to superirresponsible behavior on the latter's behalf. For example, the more the parents rescued Liz from experiencing the consequences of her truancy from school by interceding with powerful school officials, the more she skipped detentions and school. Despite the parental changes, Liz was having grave difficulty maintaining marijuana abstinence. She would go for 3 days and then use marijuana 1 or 2 days of the week. In brainstorming with Liz what resources she had outside the family that we could utilize for relapse prevention, she mentioned "three close friends" who were reformed "drug addicts." Together, we decided that it might be useful to bring in her friends to the next session, pending her parents' approval, to see what creative ideas they might have for "staying straight."

Liz's parents also thought this was a great idea. Because Liz's parents knew the parents of two of the peers, her parents agreed to call them to get approval for their daughters' participation in the next therapy session. Liz decided on her own accord to meet with the third friend's parents to discuss the situation and have them get in contact with her own parents.

Because the probation officer and school social worker were very involved with Liz's case, the family and I thought it would be a good idea to include these key members of the problem system in our future sessions as well. In the first interview, I had secured signatures on release of information forms from the family in order to collaborate with these concerned helpers.

In the third session, both the probation officer and school social worker reported noticing some important changes in Liz's behavior. According to the probation officer, Liz was "putting forth more effort" and "showing more responsible behavior." The school social worker shared with us that Liz "clearly had a better attitude" and was "attending school regularly." Despite all of Liz's changes, the parents, the probation officer, and school social worker were all very concerned about her inability to "stay straight." Earlier in the session, I had introduced Liz's three friends—Sara, Linda, and Holly—to the parents and helpers. Both the probation officer and school social worker agreed that NA was not for everyone and they were open to the idea of using Liz's peers for relapse prevention purposes. At this point in the interview, I had the peers share their ideas about how they could help Liz "stay straight." Sara began the discussion by sharing with us her story about how "keeping busy" during her leisure time was the key to how she "protected" her sobriety. Linda reported to the group that she found "aerobics" to be a great "natural high" activity. Linda got a laugh out of the group by sharing how she was "now addicted to aerobics!" Holly shared with the group that she now stays away from the "stoners [drug abusers] at school" and also avoids "going to parties." I thanked the peers for their "helpful words of wisdom" and complimented them on what "caring friends" they were. After giving the peers compliments for their helpful consultation, we decided to give Liz and her friends 3 weeks to plan out a relapse prevention strategy that would be carefully tailored to Liz's lifestyle.

During the 3-week interval, Liz was doing aerobics classes twice a week, not allowing herself one free minute during her leisure time to think about using marijuana, and she was avoiding the temptation to interact with any of her "partying" friends. At the next scheduled family–multiple helper meeting, the school social worker, probation officer, the parents, and the peers all reported marked changes in Liz's behavior. Liz was following her parent's rules, maintaining her drug abstinence, going to school regularly and keeping up with her homework, and was looking for a part-time job after school. Liz gave her friends a big hug in the session and acknowledged how instrumental they were in helping her change.

Because the probation officer and I had a close working relationship, he allowed me to determine the frequency of visits and the duration of therapy. As a group we all agreed that three future check-up sessions over the remainder of Liz's 9-month probation period would be useful to further consolidate family gains. By the last check-up session, Liz had secured a part-time job, picked up her grades, and best of all, she had remained drug-free with the help of her friends!

LIVING ON THE EDGE

Nichole, a 16-year-old acting-out adolescent, had been referred to me by her probation officer for shoplifting, substance abuse, school truancy, sexual promiscuity with older males, and chronically violating her mother's rules. Betty, Nichole's mother, had been divorced from her father for 5 years. Nichole had had very little contact with her father after the parental divorce. According to Betty, her ex-husband was a "cocaine addict." Nichole's 14-year-old brother Bill was a "jock" at school and had no behavioral difficulties.

I began my first family interview exploring with Betty and Nichole their understanding of how and why they were referred to me. I also invited each family member to share her individual stories about the family drama. Betty was quick to point out how Nichole had a "bad attitude," "never follows" her "rules," was "not going to school," and was a "thief." According to Betty, Nichole had a long history of "stealing money" from her and she was recently "arrested" at a department store for "trying to steal clothes." Nichole agreed with her mother that it was this most recent shoplifting incident that led to her being placed on probation for 1 year. Nichole further added that she hated the special therapeutic day school that she was "forced to attend" because they were "always on [her] case about everything."

Throughout the family interview, Nichole and Betty got into some heated arguments. Betty was angry at Nichole for "not coming home the other night" and for "not going to school." Nichole was angry at her mother for "always yelling" at her and not giving her a "weekly allowance." Betty also disclosed that she felt family counseling was a "waste of time" because it has "never helped in the past."

I asked the family to share with me what they liked and disliked about their three past counseling experiences. The family offered me some helpful advice about what I needed to do differently with them as a therapist.

At this point in the interview, I decided to spend some individual session time with Betty and Nichole. While meeting alone with Betty, I was able to provide support, hear more about the family story and her concerns, and elicit from her an initial treatment goal. Betty wanted Nichole to stop "ditching" school. During my individual session time with Nichole, I explored how I could be helpful to her with Betty and the school situation. Nichole disclosed that she would not steal from her mother if she got a "weekly allowance." She also reported not liking the probation officer always "checking up" on her at the school and his making "surprise visits at the house." I offered to help get the probation officer off Nichole's back because of my good relationship with him. Nichole appeared to warm up to this helpful service I could provide for her. I also shared with her that I would be glad to go to bat for her with Betty to try and negotiate the privilege of earning a weekly allowance. I shared with Nichole that I could only pursue these activities if she were willing to attend school more regularly. Nichole took a risk and shared with me what some of the major stressors at school were for her. She reported several negative encounters she had had with the school principal, the social worker, her teacher Mrs. Smith, and some rival gang members who also attended the school. I provided support and asked Nichole if she thought it might be helpful for me to advocate for her at the school. Nichole thought it was "worth a try" to collaborate with the school staff.

To close out the first family interview, I provided compliments for both Betty and Nichole and conducted a macrosystemic assessment with them. The family felt it would be in their best interest for me to collaborate with the school principal, the social worker, Mrs. Smith, and the probation officer. I had Betty and Nichole sign consent forms so I could collaborate with these key members of the problem system.

Present at the first school meeting were the probation officer, the principal, the social worker, and Mrs. Smith. I began the meeting by inviting the school staff to share their stories about Nichole and her family. For the majority of the meeting time, each school representative had nothing but negative and pathology-laden stories to tell about Betty and Nichole. The principal called Nichole "unmotivated," a "sociopath," and in need of "psychiatric hospitalization." In fact, he had been making arrangements with the school's psychiatric consultant to try to have Nichole admitted at a local psychiatric hospital. According to the school social worker, Nichole's mother was "neglectful," "irresponsible," and had "failed several" of their "scheduled appointments." Mrs. Smith felt that Nichole had an "I don't care" attitude about school and herself. While I was listening to the school staff members' stories of hopelessness about this family, I began to wonder whether it would be possible to establish a collaborative relationship with them. The school staff seemed ready to throw in the towel with Nichole and her family.

Despite my discomfort with the school staff's stories about Nichole and her mother, I could empathize with their dilemma of having to work with students with long histories of behavioral difficulties, and their families. Prior to the conclusion of our meeting together, I asked if the school staff had any helpful suggestions about how we could cooperate in the therapeutic-change effort with Nichole and her mother. The school principal recommended that I have the mother "check her insurance to see if it would cover inpatient treatment for Nichole." The school social worker commented that she would be "willing to do family therapy sessions together," but that "they really don't want to change." At this point, the probation officer entered the conversation and stressed the importance of "team work" and giving Nichole "support at school." The school staff reluctantly agreed to have another meeting in 3 weeks.

While driving back to the office with the probation officer, he shared with me that in the past he had had grave difficulty establishing a collaborative working relationship with this school staff with some of his other cases. After hearing some of the probation officer's past case experiences, I no longer felt alone with my concerns about being able to enlist the school's support in the change effort. We both agreed that Nichole was "living on the edge" through her acting-out behavior, and that she was clearly one of the school's toughest students to manage.

During the 3-week interval, Nichole had gone to school almost every day and was consistently following her mother's rules. In our third family session, Nichole's behavioral progress was officially rewarded by her mother with the presentation of her first $10 weekly allowance. Nichole was thrilled and voiced a strong desire to keep up her good work. Nichole was also shocked to hear that her probation officer had advocated strongly for her in the school meeting. Hearing this important information appeared to give Nichole a different view of her probation officer and greatly contributed to their having a better working relationship. Although the family experienced a few big arguments during this break period, they confidently reported getting quickly back on track again.

In my second school meeting, there was group consensus among the school staff members and the probation officer that Nichole was making good progress. However, the school principal was quick to point out that this was a "honeymoon period," which he has seen before with Nichole. Both the social worker and Mrs. Smith agreed with the principal that Nichole's changes must be approached with "guarded optimism." I asked the school staff members if they were doing anything differently when interacting with Nichole that seemed to be helpful. Nobody reported having done anything differently when communicating with Nichole. Suprisingly, Mrs. Smith asked me if I had any suggestions of new strategies that she could try out with Nichole in the classroom. I recommended to her that she keep track of all of the various things she does with Nichole that seem to be helpful, and notice what Nichole does in the classroom that she would like to see Nichole continue. Mrs. Smith liked my suggestions and promised to have a progress report for me for the next scheduled meeting, in 3 weeks. It was also decided by the group that Nichole's mother be included in the next meeting.

One week prior to our next school meeting, Nichole's behavior took a turn for the worse. Nichole had stolen $50 from her mother, she "ditched" three days of school, and had been caught with a $10 bag of marijuana in the school bathroom. She also failed to come home for two nights. According to Betty, she was out "whoring around" with some older teenagers. There were also rumors around the school that she had asked two of her gang-involved friends to slice the principal's car tires. The probation officer had phoned me to say that he had no alternative but to have Nichole placed in the juvenile detention center for 1 month.

In my fourth and fifth family sessions with Nichole and her

mother, I did not see or hear any indications that she was heading for a major behavioral relapse. While Nichole was in the juvenile detention center, I visited her two times. On both occasions, Nichole appeared to be depressed and remorseful. I also discovered in our second visit together that Nichole's mother had agreed to allow her to drop out of school, providing that she would work.

After Nichole was released from the detention center, she was court-ordered to continue family therapy. Nichole was expected to look for a job actively, do chores around the house, and follow her mother's rules. For additional support, I put Nichole in contact with two former adolescent clients who had also been on probation and had drastically changed their situations and become responsible young people. Not only did these two female peers help Nichole secure a job at a fast-food restaurant, but they all became close friends.

At times in future family sessions I included the probation officer and the peers. Our teamwork helped Nichole successfully terminate her probation.

TEACHER POWER

Todd, 14 years old, was referred for family therapy because of his failing grades, poor "frustration tolerance level, temper outbursts, frequent confrontations with teachers, and inability to respond to the teachers' limit setting." According to the school social worker, Todd had a long history of behavioral problems while in junior high. After receiving Todd's mother's verbal consent on the telephone to talk to the school social worker, I called the latter to gather more detailed information about the presenting problems and the school's attempted solutions. I recommended to the school social worker that it would be useful to set up a meeting with Todd's six teachers so that we could collaborate on the case. I also shared with him that I would need to get the parent's and Todd's written consent in order to collaborate with the school.

In my first family therapy session, I met with Todd, his younger brother, Steve, and his parents. According to the parents, Todd did not have major behavioral problems at home, but would occasionally get "too physically rough" with Steve and also tested parental limits. We discussed the parent's and Todd's perspectives on the school difficulties. The parents were quick to share with me that Todd had an IQ of 130 and used to get A's and B's in all of his subjects before entering junior high. Over the past school year, however, Todd reportedly was receiving F's in his math, English, and social studies classes. The teachers in each of these classes had frequent phone contacts with Todd's mother regarding his temper outbursts, inability to respond to their limits, confrontations, and failing grades. Todd reported that his teachers were "mean" and quite "rigid" with him. He cited one example of his English teacher's rigid behavior around turning in an assignment 1 day late and receiving an F on his paper. Both Todd and his parents gave me written consent to collaborate with the school social worker and the teachers.

At my first school consultation were Todd's six teachers, the school social worker, and the school principal. After I established rapport with each individual at the meeting, I asked the school social worker to share how he viewed Todd's situation and his decision to refer the case to me. I learned from the social worker that Todd "weekly" visited the "principal's office" for disciplinary reasons and that he frequently "blew off" his scheduled counseling appointments. Todd's English teacher was quite outspoken about what a "troublemaker" Todd was. She claimed he was a very "emotionally troubled young man." The math teacher reported that Todd was a "difficult student" and the "class clown." His social studies teacher saw similar behaviors in his class. At this point in the meeting, I explored with Todd's gym, art, and science teachers their observations of Todd and how he was functioning in their classes.

Surprisingly, these three teachers viewed Todd as a "dynamic, bright, and hard-working young man." They reported how "cooperative" and "responsible" Todd was in their classrooms. I also discovered that Todd was receiving A's and B's in their classes. In the context of this discussion, the English teacher inquired of the more positive teachers what their "secret" was for "making Todd behave so well." The art teacher shared with the other teachers that it was important to be "laid back with Todd" and "avoid putting pressure on him." The science teacher agreed with this strategy and further stressed the need to "accentuate Todd's strengths." The gym teacher shared with the group that Todd has "great leadership abilities" and he found that by capitalizing on this strength, he "earned Todd's cooperation."

While sitting in the meeting observing this productive cross-fertilization of ideas between the teachers, I was amazed by their creativity and problem-solving abilities. There was a strong sense of community among the six teachers, despite the fact that they had never sat together to brainstorm about how to best manage Todd in the classroom and to share their differing opinions about my client.

By the end of the first school meeting, the first group, the English, math, and social studies teachers, were eager to try out some of the new strategies they had learned from their colleagues. The art, science, and gym teachers (the second group) asked me if I had any suggestions for things they could do as well. I reminded the second group that "if it works, don't fix it" and encouraged them to "do more of the same" with Todd. As an experiment, I offered the first group the following task to do between this consultation session and our next scheduled meeting: "Keep track of all of the things that Todd does that you want to continue to see in your classrooms. Also, keep track of what you do that works with Todd." I asked the teachers to "write those things down and be prepared to discuss them in our next meeting." We also all agreed that Todd and his parents should attend our future meetings. The second school meeting was scheduled for 3 weeks later.

Two days after the school consultation, I met with Todd and his parents. Todd's mother reported that she had noticed that her son was "doing his homework." I shared with the parents and Todd what had been discussed in the school meeting. While meeting alone with Todd in the family session, I gave Todd the following task to do over the next 3 weeks: "Each day at school, I would like you to notice two things that your English, math, and social studies teachers do that you like, write those things down, and report those good things to your mother daily." Earlier in the session, I had shared with the parents my plans to give this task to Todd with the rationale that it could "help improve" their son's "relationships with his teachers." Todd's mother planned to buy a notebook to record her son's daily discoveries.

At the next school meeting, all six of Todd's teachers had nothing but praise for his great progress. The biggest surprise for the parents, myself, and the school social worker, was hearing the English teacher's report about how well Todd was "performing" in her classroom. He was being "more respectful" towards her and "turning in his assignments on time." Todd shared with the English teacher that he had noticed that she was "nicer" to him. Both the math and social studies teachers also reported Todd's "considerable progress" academically and behaviorally. I spent the majority of this meeting amplifying the changes reported by the teachers and Todd. The parents thanked the teachers for being so "committed" to trying to help Todd out. Todd shared with the teachers and school social worker that he would continue to work on improving his grades and behavior. By the end of the meeting, it was decided that I would see the family two more times over the school year to monitor progress.

No further difficulties were reported by the school or the

parents at each of our check-up sessions. Todd ended up finishing the school year with a B+ grade-point average.

CONCLUSION

In each of the case examples described in this chapter, I attempted to cocreate a safe dialogical space with the families and involved helpers in which everyone's voice was heard and the generation of new narratives and creative solutions was possible. As can be seen with all five case examples, through mobilizing and collaborating with the key resource people in the adolescents' social ecologies, therapeutic changes were not only coproduced rapidly, but were also quite dramatic.

S I X

KEEPING CHANGE RIPPLING ON: PRESCRIPTION FOR THE SECOND AND SUBSEQUENT SESSIONS

To persist, the new must be such a sort that it will endure longer than the alternatives. What lasts longer among the ripples of the random must last longer than those ripples that last not so long. . . .
—GREGORY BATESON discussing how new ideas endure over time in living systems (1980, p. 50)

In the second and subsequent sessions, our main job as brief therapists is to actively amplify and consolidate family changes in such a way that these differences become more "newsworthy" to the family and continue to ripple on long after therapy is completed. When families return for their second sessions, there are four common positions they will present with that are based on the impact of the new ideas and therapeutic tasks they received in the first interview. These four positions are as follows: *better, mixed opinion, same,* or *worse.* In this chapter, I will discuss therapeutic guidelines for task design and selection with each of these client positions, creative uses of the consultation team, and end of therapy rituals to celebrate therapeutic changes. Case examples will be provided throughout the chapter.

TASK DESIGN AND SELECTION FOR VARIOUS CLIENT POSITIONS

BETTER FAMILIES

When families present for the second and subsequent sessions with significant changes in their goal area or in other areas, I spend the majority of the session amplifying the exceptions and consolidating the family gains. Through the use of cheerleading, exception-oriented questions, and highlighting differences with unique account and redescription questions (White, 1988b), I help make these important changes "newsworthy" to the family. When cheerleading I give family members high fives and handshakes, and respond to each exception with questions like: "How did you do that!?"; "How did you get that to happen!?"; "How did you come up with that clever idea!?"; "Is that different!?" It is helpful to have family members make distinctions between their old patterns of behavior and their new patterns of interaction. I use consolidating and presuppositional questions (O'Hanlon & Weiner-Davis, 1989) to reinforce the new exception patterns of behavior. Some useful consolidating questions to ask for reinforcing and amplifying family changes are as follows: "What would you have to do to go backwards?"; "What would you have to do to prevent a major backslide?"; "What will you have to continue to do to get that [exception behavior] to happen more often?"; "If we were to gaze into my imaginary crystal ball three months down the road, what further changes will we see happening in this family?" As another way to highlight differences, I may also check with the parents and the identified client as to how they presently rate themselves on the scale of their goal area.

Therapeutic Task Design and Selection

Some families will not request further therapy visits due to their significant changes or problem resolution. In this instance, I take an intersession break to "meet with myself" to construct compliments for family members or I have the team come into the therapy room to reflect their compliments and ideas to the family and I behind the one-way mirror. If the latter format is used, I have the family provide their reflections on the team's reflections and terminate therapy. I always tell families that I have an "open door" policy if they ever need to come in for a future "tune-up" session. I follow the same open door format if I am working solo.

Other families may wish to continue in therapy in order to do further work in their goal area. Besides having the team reflect their compliments and ideas to the family at the intersession break, I assess with the family whether they would like to continue using the same homework assignment they were given in the first session or if they would like to try a new task. The team and I share with the family our bias for doing more of what works by telling them, "We believe if it works, don't fix it" (de Shazer, 1985). If the parents request a different task, the team and I may recommend to them an observation task (Molnar & de Shazer, 1987) so that they will "continue to notice what further changes they will make." We may also offer the adolescent the "secret surprise" task (O'Hanlon & Weiner-Davis, 1989) during individual session time. During that session, I ask the adolescent to pick two surprises to do over the week or during the break period between sessions that will shock the parents in a positive way. The adolescent cannot tell the parents what the surprises were. The parents are instructed to pull out their magnifying glasses like Sherlock Holmes and Mata Hari and look for what those surprises might be that will "shock them in a positive way."

Longer Time Intervals

My colleagues and I have found it useful to give families longer time intervals between sessions as a vote of confidence. We increasingly add longer periods of time between sessions until the family feels more confident to make a go of it on their own. Palazzoli and her colleagues (1980) found that giving families longer time intervals between sessions gave the families more time to think about the new ideas introduced by the therapist and the consultation team. At the same time, longer time intervals between sessions can provide ample time for family members to notice differences and changes occurring within their family situations. With court-referred families that have been committed to seeing me for a year by the probation officer or the judge, I do *brief long-term therapy*. Once I have negotiated with the probation officer or the judge, I may see a family six times over an entire year. I have also found the brief long-term therapy strategy useful with some chronic substance abusers and eating disorder clients because it serves to strengthen the clients' natural coping skills for successfully managing inevitable future slips. I call these future scheduled visits "tune-up" sessions.

MIXED OPINION FAMILIES

When families return for their second session, reporting concerns about the goal area or other difficulties that occurred in 1 week's time, I begin the interview by asking the family about the times when the difficulties were *not* occurring. When exception material is produced, I amplify these changes through cheerleading and exception-oriented questions. If this strategy works, I utilize presuppositional questions to move the family into a future reality without problems. I use either my imaginary crystal ball (de Shazer, 1985) or my videotape metaphor (O'Hanlon & Weiner-Davis, 1989) to achieve this end. I may also explore with the parents and the identified client where they presently rank themselves on the scale of goal attainment.

If the above stategy leads to the negation of exceptions by

the parents, I do something different by asking them: "How come things are not worse?" Oftentimes parents respond to this question with important exception material. With every exception that is reported to me, I respond with cheerleading and exception-oriented questions. The original treatment goal established by the family may also need to be examined and renegotiated into a smaller, more solvable goal.

Therapeutic Task Design and Selection

Besides giving compliments and sharing some of our ideas with the family, the team and I offer the family a new therapeutic task that better fits with their unique cooperative response pattern. The "do something different task" (de Shazer, 1985) is particularly useful with parents that are stuck doing "more of the same" (Watzlawick et al., 1974). If the exceptions appear to be happening spontaneously without any explanations for their occurrence, the team and I might use the prediction task (de Shazer, 1988) or some other task that can be performed on a random basis. With parents who are concerned that the identified client's may have future relapses or difficulties, the team and I share that "change is three steps forward and two steps back, but we will not be back to square one" (de Shazer, 1985).

Case Example: Roger

Roger, 16 years old, was brought to therapy by his parents for chronic rule violation, police involvement, and school truancy. The parents decided in the first interview that they wished for the "school attendance problem" to change. According to the parents, Roger would cut a few days of school with his "friends" and then attend 1 or 2 days per week. Neither the parents nor Roger could explain these spontaneous exceptions. Throughout the interview, I observed that the parents were highly conflictual and frequently put down each other's parenting styles in relationship to Roger. I used exception-oriented questions and had Roger leave the room which seemed to help short-circuit this vicious pattern of interaction. After complimenting each family member on their strengths and coping strategies, I offered the family the prediction task (de Shazer, 1988) as a "useful experiment" for the week. Each night the threesome were to separately predict whether Roger would be "staying in school" the next day and then, the next day, to account for why this happened.

The family returned to the second session reporting that Roger had "gone to school four out of five days." I pulled out my imaginary pom-poms and cheered, and also amplified the exceptions. However, the parents began to criticize one another on how they had handled a "big blowup" about Roger. Roger had wanted to go to a party with some of his "troublemaking friends" and his mother had told him "No!" The father, on the other hand, felt it would have been "okay for Roger to go" to the party. I asked Roger to sit in the lobby while I met alone with the parents. I complimented each parent on doing a fine job of getting Roger to "stay in school." I decided to give the parents an observation task for the next week in which each parent would separately observe what the other does about Roger that they liked and jot those things down so we could discuss their discoveries in the next session. The parents agreed with me that they "spent too little" time acknowledging "the good things" they each did with their son. After complimenting each family member, I recommended that they continue to do the prediction task with the rationale of "keep doing more of what works."

One week later, the family came in reporting a wealth of exceptions. Roger was going to "school daily," there were "no blowups," and the parents had not criticized or argued with one another for the entire week. When I met alone with the parents, each parent reported at least four things that they liked about the other's parenting abilities. As a vote of confidence to the family, I gave them a 4-week vacation from therapy. While on vacation, I asked them to "continue doing more of what works." We mutually decided to terminate therapy after the vacation break, due to problem resolution.

SAME FAMILIES

When families report no further improvement in the second and subsequent sessions, I first explore whether there was at least one good day over the course of the week and attempt to amplify its exceptions. It is important to secure detailed information about all of the exceptions that occurred on the one good day because they may serve as potential building blocks for solution construction. If my exception-oriented inquiry produces negative client feedback, I explore with the family how they prevented things from getting worse. If the family is still negative and pessimistic about their situation, I take this as important client feedback indicating that I need to do something therapeutically different. To begin with, it is helpful to keep things simple by investigating some basic areas with the family, such as whether we have a well-formed treatment goal or a customer. Whenever I feel we are stuck, I assess with the family whether our treatment goal is too monolithic and needs to be broken down further, or whether we selected the wrong goal area to begin working on first. I may try utilizing the pessimistic sequence (Berg & Gallagher, 1991) to help generate some exceptions. I also explore with the family whether anyone else needs to be participating in our therapy sessions who is not presently involved. In assessing customership with the family, I may ask the identified client to rank on a scale from 1 to 10, 10 being most concerned, all family members and significant others not present in our sessions at the time. The answer to this question often provides me with important clues as to who I need to include in future sessions. While assessing customership, I may want to conduct a macrosystemic assessment (Selekman & Todd, 1991) with the family to invite them to tell me what involved helpers from larger systems I need to collaborate with as well. If there are multiple helpers involved in the family case, I secure signed release of information forms from the family and recommend that we have family–multiple helper meetings in the future.

Therapeutic Task Design and Selection

With some families, when I shift gears and ask, "How come things are not worse?," some important exceptions will be produced, which can be utilized as building blocks toward co-constructing a solution with the family. The pessimistic sequence (Berg & Gallagher, 1991) can be utilized if no exceptions are produced. If the family continues to be pessimistic, I may shift gears and ask them to give me a videotape description of the problem-maintaining sequence of interaction in the family. Pattern intervention (O'Hanlon, 1987; O'Hanlon & Weiner-Davis, 1989) is an effective therapeutic strategy for disrupting the problem-maintaining sequences of interaction in the family. O'Hanlon (1987) has developed a useful guide for how to disrupt problem-maintaining patterns in the client system. Some of his recommendations are as follows:

1. Change the frequency/rate of the symptom/symptom-pattern.
2. Change the duration of the symptom/symptom-pattern.
3. Change the time (of day/week/month/year) of the symptom/symptom-pattern.
4. Change the location of the symptom/symptom-pattern.
5. Add or subtract (at least) one element to or from the sequence.
6. Change the sequence (order) of events around the symptom. (p. 36)

If the family warms up to the idea of experimenting with a task that the team and I wish to offer them, we will pursue the pattern intervention route with the family.

Case Example: Rorie

Rorie had been sent to me for family therapy by his school counselor for drug abuse and school truancy. Rorie refused to come to the first family session. I used the majority of the first session exploring parental exceptions and helpful past attempted solutions. The parents could not identify any exceptions or useful strategies that they had utilized to get Rorie to go to school or curtail his marijuana use. Even asking the miracle question (de Shazer, 1988) and cooperating with their pessimistic stance failed to generate any exception material. Because the parents spent the majority of the session time complaining about Rorie's behavior, I decided to offer them an observation task (Molnar & de Shazer, 1987). The parents liked the idea of spending the week observing, rather than "wasting" their time "yelling at Rorie."

One week later, the parents returned reporting no exceptions in Rorie's behavior. At this point, I decided to shift gears and track the problem-maintaining sequence around Rorie's marijuana abuse. The parents wanted to change the marijuana problem first. I asked the mother to give me a videotaped description of what happens prior to, during, and after Rorie uses marijuana at home. The mother's videotaped description was as follows: Rorie comes home around 4:00 P.M. probably "high" on drugs; "blasts his music" and "smokes more marijuana in his bedroom," sometimes alone or with friends; she confronts Rorie, Rorie "screams" at her; "Rorie storms out of the house"; father comes home and the parents take away Rorie's "stereo and telephone" for a period of time; Rorie comes home around 9:00 or 10:00 P.M. and he "locks himself up" in his room; and the parents tell Rorie that he is "grounded" for the upcoming weekend.

The parents were at their wits end. They were unable to enforce any of their consequences with Rorie. The parents turned to me and asked me if I had "any new ideas" for them. Because the parents were willing to try anything at this point and finances were not an issue for them, I suggested that they hire two local actors dressed as FBI agents to come by the house at 4:00 P.M. The actors were to be told to pretend that they were investigating a drug-dealing ring in the neighborhood and that they wanted to question Rorie. They were to take Rorie for a ride in their car and to point out that he was a potential suspect. The parents loved this idea and went to work the following week to call local acting agencies.

Two weeks later, after hiring two actors and coaching them on their roles, the parents decided to test out this strategy on a Wednesday at 4:00 P.M. According to the parents, the strategy had a profound impact on Rorie's behavior. Not only was he "scared out of his mind," but the following changes occurred: Rorie was "going to school"; he no longer "showed any signs of marijuana use"; his music was "not being blasted"; and he was "following" the parental "rules." Rorie also attended our three remaining therapy sessions. Both the parents and I pretended that the FBI investigation was a serious concern for Rorie. Rorie was willing to do anything to get off the FBI's suspect list, such as "remaining drug-free" and "going to school." I also collaborated with concerned school personnel to further assist Rorie in his quest to turn over a new leaf at school. Rorie gave up his marijuana abuse and school truancy behaviors after discovering the "serious consequences" of his "actions" and learning that he could earn "nice privileges" by "staying out of further trouble."

Some families, however, return to the second and subsequent sessions feeling highly pessimistic and victimized by the presenting problem. Many of these families have experienced multiple treatment failures and have been oppressed by the problem for a long time. Besides exploring what previous therapists might have overlooked or missed with them (storytelling), I externalize the problem (White & Epston, 1990). The team and I develop an experiment for the family designed to help empower them to go to combat against the oppressive problem.

Case Example: Steve

The Andrews sought therapy for their 17-year-old son, Steve, who had a long history of abusing drugs. Steve had been in two drug rehabilitation programs in the past and relapsed shortly after being discharged from the last program. Mr. Andrews viewed Steve as being "a druggie" because he refused to "stay straight." Mrs. Andrews felt that Steve had been "trying harder lately" to change. Steve shared in the first interview that kids at school were calling him a "stoner" and "fry brain," which "pissed" him off. Steve's older brother, who was away at college, also had had a problem with drugs when he was in high school. My attempt to elicit exception material from the parents was met with negativity and pessimism. I quickly moved to asking the family the miracle question (de Shazer, 1988). The parents miracles were Steve's maintaining drug abstinence, Steve and his father "getting along better," "less arguing" in the family, and Steve staying away from his "partying friends." I decided to meet alone with Steve to further develop my therapeutic alliance with him. I offered him two homework assignments due to his high level of motivation to do something about his drug problem. The first assignment was for Steve to notice all of the various things he would do to avoid the temptation to get "buzzed" (Steve's language) over the next week (de Shazer, 1985) and to write those things down for the next session. The second task was for Steve to pick 2 days over the next week to pretend to engage in miracle behaviors (de Shazer, 1991) so we could "blow" his "parents' minds!" After giving the family compliments, I asked the parents to pull out their imaginary magnifying glasses and try to guess days on which Steve was pretending to engage in miracle behaviors.

One week later, the family returned reporting minimal changes and were quite negative. An argument erupted in the session between Steve and his father over the former's not "wanting to change." I disrupted this destructive blaming cycle through externalizing the problem (White & Epston, 1990). I asked the family the following externalizing questions: "How long has the 'druggie' lifestyle been pushing your sons around?"; "What kinds of things did you do to help Bill [the older brother] escape from the 'druggie' lifestyle?"; "Steve, how long are you going to allow the 'druggie' lifestyle to invite the kids at school to call you a 'stoner' or 'fry brain?' " The atmosphere in the room greatly changed and my externalizing questions seemed to open up space for family members to view the problem situation differently. The parents began to talk about how this was a family problem. They had remembered that when Bill was grappling with the "druggie" lifestyle, they made a conscious effort to stop blaming him, which "seemed to work" in helping him change. Steve responded to my question about how he invites the "druggie" lifestyle to make the peers at school call him a "stoner" and "fry brain" with a lot of emotion. Steve commented: "I'm sick of those assholes!"; "I'm sick of being called a 'stoner' and 'fry brain!' "

Because I had no team, I took a break to "meet with myself" to design an appropriate task to offer the family. Each day family members were to keep track of the various things they did to stand up to the "druggie" lifestyle and not allow it to push them around, both at home and at school. The family was also instructed to meet after dinner for a half an hour to discuss their daily victories over the "druggie" lifestyle, what specifically they were doing to stand up to it, as well as how they were being pushed around by it. I explained to the family that "druggie" lifestyles do not die easily, so that the evening meetings were essential for strategizing and support. I asked the family whether they wanted to come back in 2 or 3 weeks. The family decided to come back in 2 weeks.

Two weeks later, the parents and Steve came in smiling and in good spirits. Steve had remained "straight" for "two weeks!" I fell out of my chair when Steve reported his tremendous accomplishment. There had been "no arguments" during the break period. The father, who was a Cubs baseball fan, said, "Steve was batting a thousand!" Steve's mother reported that she had seen him "doing his homework," which was a "big change." Steve reported that he found it useful to meet with his parents nightly for support and that he had steered clear of his "partying friends." After highlighting differences and amplifying the multitude of family changes, I recommended that they continue doing the task and that we meet again in 4 weeks as a vote of confidence to the family. I ended up seeing Steve's family two more times. For the last session, which was 2 months after the third session, I bought a cake to celebrate the Andrews' victory over the "druggie" lifestyle.

Managing Temporary Family Derailments

While on longer time intervals or mini-vacations from therapy, families may experience some slipping back from their improvement in the goal area or a fall back into their old problem-maintaining patterns of interaction, in response to a relapse. Once notified by the parents, I call the family in for an immediate tune-up session. After normalizing the slip as a temporary derailment and an opportunity for comeback practice (Tomm & White, 1987), I explore with the family the steps they have already taken prior to our tune-up session to get back on track again. If the family is still in crisis or feeling derailed, I ask the following questions: "What will you have to do to get back on track again?"; "What will you have to do to stay on track?"; "What will you do to get that to happen?"; "What else will you have to do more of to get back on track again?" I may bring out my imaginary crystal ball (de Shazer, 1985) and have family members describe what they will be doing at a future time to remain on track. By the end of the tune-up session if there are still some minor concerns, I schedule a future appointment and send the family back on their vacation from therapy as a vote of confidence in them.

WORSE FAMILIES

When families return for the second and subsequent sessions reporting that their problem situation has gotten worse, I respond to this important client feedback by doing something different therapeutically. The pessimistic sequence (Berg & Gallagher, 1991) may be a useful pathway to pursue to help foster a better cooperative relationship.

Besides assessing with the family if we need a smaller or new treatment goal, I also explore with them who else we need to have present in our therapy sessions, including involved helpers from larger systems. If the family has not responded well to Solution-Oriented tasks or pattern intervention (O'Hanlon, 1987), I externalize the problem (White & Epston, 1990). With some families, however, the small changes that the above strategies might have produced are not differences that make a difference to the family. Therefore, with these families it can be quite useful to intervene less and to give them more room to tell their problem-saturated stories. Asking conversational questions (Anderson & Goolishian, 1988a), can open up space for family members to tell their story without any editing on the therapist and team's behalf. This can lead to new narratives and meanings being generated by family members about their family story.

Case Example: Kelly

Kelly, 17 years old, was court-ordered to therapy for shoplifting, chronic violation of parental rules, school truancy, and substance abuse. In the first session, the team and I recommended to the parents the "do something different task" (de Shazer, 1985). One week later, the family returned reporting no progress at all. In fact, Kelly's acting-out behavior had gotten worse. The parents' goal for Kelly was for her to "come home on time at least one time" over the next week. Kelly would not commit to her parent's goal and could not identify anything she really wanted to get out of therapy or from her parents. According to the parents, Kelly had not come home on time once and they were "furious at her." I tracked the problem sequence and discovered that the major family arguments occurred in the kitchen after Kelly returned home late at night. Kelly usually won these family arguments because she was "more awake" than her parents. She typically ended up cussing them out and locking herself up in her bedroom. The team and I recommended to the family that they schedule their family arguments in the living room earlier in the evening when the parents were "more awake." Our rationale for having the family arguments was that this was the best way each family member could convey their "concern and emotional connection" to one another. We instructed them to take turns arguing with one family member at a time for 5 minutes. They were to use the kitchen timer in order to accurately keep track of the time. Any leftover topics to argue about were to be written down on a piece of paper and used in the next scheduled arguing session.

When the family returned for our third session, they reported a major decrease in the family arguments and some behavioral improvement with Kelly. I amplified all of the changes. However, Kelly looked depressed and was shaking in her chair. There seemed to be some tension between Kelly and her father. The team picked up on these important nonverbals and commented on them as part of their reflection when the family and I went behind the one-way mirror at the intersession break. Some of the team's reflections were as follows: "I wonder if there is some missing piece to this family puzzle that has not yet been talked about?"; "Yeah, despite all of the family's progress over the past week, there seems to be something that is putting a damper on the good feelings . . ."; "I wonder if Kelly is trying to tell us something, like what the missing piece of the family puzzle might be, but is not sure how the piece will fit for them as a family . . ."

After we switched rooms, the family reflected on the team's reflections. Kelly surprisingly took a risk and shared with us that her 24-year-old brother, who was home from college for the summer, had sexually abused her 3 years ago. The parents were totally shocked, particularly the father, who was very close to his son. According to Kelly, Alan (the older brother) had come home drunk from a party while the parents were out for the evening and forced her to have intercourse with him. Alan had threatened to "kill" her if she "spilled the beans." The mother hugged Kelly and told her that "this will never happen again" and "Alan will be dealt with." The father planned to confront Alan about the sex abuse incident and make him "go for therapy." The parents denied knowing anything about their daughter's sexual victimization. I shared with the family that, because I am a mandated reporter, we would have to call the child protective services department and report this incident. The father offered to call from my office. I told the family that I would collaborate with the child protective service worker and provide advocacy and family therapy for them during this crisis period.

Kelly and her parents decided to press charges against Alan. He was court-ordered to a sex offender's group. Future family sessions involved providing support for Kelly and her family and collaborating with the child protective service worker and the probation officer. I saw Kelly and her parents six more times. I also got Kelly into a special group for sexually abused girls. Kelly's behavior dramatically improved after her courageous disclosure to her parents.

Kelly's case is an excellent example of the importance of therapeutic flexibility. The team and I began therapy utilizing the basic Solution-Oriented Brief Therapy approach which failed to produce any significant changes in the family—in fact, things had gotten worse. We attempted to disrupt the problem-maintaining pattern of interaction around Kelly's breaking curfew, which produced some changes, but they were not "newsworthy" to her because she had an important story to tell. Our original highly interventionistic and intentional therapeutic stance blocked Kelly from telling her story. It was clear that we needed to do something different. The reflecting team members picked up on some important nonverbals that were indicative of some family secret being hidden. They were free as a group to talk metaphorically about the family secret from a meta-position, which paved the way for Kelly to disclose the "not yet said" (Anderson & Goolishian, 1988b). Kelly's courageous disclosure helped generate new meaning for the parents regarding her behavior and led to very dramatic family changes.

DISCONNECTED FAMILIES

With some families, a change in one part of the family system fails to produce changes in the other parts of the system. Family members and subsystems in these families tend to be disconnected from one another. In some cases, even altering the concerned parent's behavior in relationship to the adolescent does not produce change, but tends to reinforce the adolescent's symptoms or further exacerbates them. I have witnessed this phenomenon with families in which there were multiple symptom-bearers. One useful therapeutic strategy with disconnected families is to intervene separately through family members or subsystems. I establish separate treatment goals with family members and encourage them to do things differently with one another. A former disconnected family case of mine illustrates how challenging these cases are to work with.

Case Example: Wendy

Sarah had brought her alcohol-abusing 17-year-old daughter, Wendy, in for therapy "out of fear" that she "will fail her senior year" of high school because of her heavy alcohol abuse. After three sessions of therapy, Wendy's alcohol abuse behavior and school problems got worse, despite Sarah's making remarkable changes, such as going to Al-Anon and not being superresponsible in relation to Wendy. I had failed to engage Wendy in the first interview and she had decided to boycott our future therapy sessions. Because I was feeling "stuck" and I was teamless for this case, I decided to expand the system and have Sarah bring her husband and 26-year-old son to the next session. The father came to our next session smelling of alcohol and looking dishevelled. Wendy's older brother had been arrested for cocaine dealing prior to our session. My attempts to engage the father proved to be futile. Sarah and I ended up having four more sessions together. She continued to go to Al-Anon for support, stopped being "super mom," and began taking evening college classes. Sarah eventually came to the realization in therapy that the only person that could change in her family was herself.

Although I failed to resolve Sarah's presenting complaint, I still consider this case to be a therapeutic success. Sarah took many courageous steps in therapy to empower herself and learn how to better cope with a very troubling family situation. In our last session together, I complimented her on successfully "mastering the art of detachment" and for utilizing the "Serenity Prayer's" wisdom to better cope with her family.

SOLUTION-ORIENTED TASKS AND TEAM STRATEGIES

In this section of the chapter, I will present ten Solution-Oriented therapeutic tasks and team strategies that I have found to be useful with difficult adolescents and their families. I will describe each therapeutic task and team strategy, offer helpful guidelines about when to utilize them in the treatment process, and provide some case examples.

COIN FLIP

When faced with parents who have difficulties sharing disciplining responsibilities, I instruct the parents each morning to flip a coin to determine who will be completely in charge of the disciplining for the day (de Shazer, 1988). This way each parent has an equal shot at playing the "heavy" role. I have found that this therapeutic task can reduce conflict between the parents and it rebalances relations between the parents and the adolescent.

SECRET SURPRISE

The "secret surprise task" (O'Hanlon & Weiner-Davis, 1989) consists of having the adolescent pick two surprising things to do in 1 week's time to shock the parents in a positive way. The adolescent is not allowed to tell the parents what the surprises are. The parents are instructed to pull out their imaginary magnifying glasses and try to identify what their adolescent's surprises were. This is a playful task that is useful for amplifying exceptions and changes. Sometimes I reverse the task and have the parents provide the secret surprises. I like to use this task with the *better* and *mixed opinion* client groups.

SOLUTION ENHANCEMENT TASK

For clients presenting with habit disorders like substance abuse and eating problems, the solution enhancement task (de Shazer, 1985) can empower them to stand up to their bad habits. The adolescent is instructed as follows: "Over the next week, I want you to notice all of the various things you will do to avoid the temptation to [client language] get 'buzzed,' 'high,' to 'pigout,' 'binge,' and so forth." This therapeutic task is useful with *mixed opinion* clients to help generate more exceptions and further enhance their problem-solving capacities. With some substance-abusing clients, I encourage them to write down their useful solutions on blank cards and carry them around in their purses and wallets. I have had some former difficult adolescent clients tell me that they have found their "solution cards" helpful to them in times of crisis.

HABIT CONTROL RITUAL

The habit control ritual (Durrant & Coles, 1991) can be useful with families that have been oppressed by a particular symptom for a long time. Once the family's symptom has been externalized, family members can be instructed to keep track on a daily basis of the various things they do to stand up to the symptom and to not allow it to get the best of them. They are also asked to keep track of the symptom's victories over them. Nightly family meetings are scheduled for strategizing purposes until the oppressive symptom has been conquered by the family. This task is particularly useful with families that are in the *same* or *worse* categories in second or subsequent sessions.

SYMBOLIC EXTERNALIZATION RITUAL

Friesen, Grigg, and Newman (1991) have expanded on Michael White's "externalization of the problem" (White & Epston, 1990) therapeutic strategy, by cocreating with the family an external symbol or metaphorical representation of their oppressive symptom. After an external symbol is selected by the family that reflects their concerns about the symptom, they are asked to describe their relationships with the symbol, and what they would like to say to it. Family members are to engage directly in dialogue with the symbol and with each other about the symbol. Any possible changes in their relationships to the symbol are explored and amplified. Finally, the therapist and family jointly decide what to do with the symbol once they have conquered it. The symbolic externalization ritual in general is useful with families that have been oppressed by a symptom for a long time, have not responded well to the basic Solution-Oriented approach, and are in the *same* or *worse* categories. The following case example illustrates the utility of this therapeutic task.

Case Example: Wally

Wally was brought to therapy by his parents for his alcohol abuse problem. His paternal grandfather had died from alcoholism and the parents were quite concerned that he was "becoming alcoholic." Wally's grades in school had greatly declined once he began drinking heavily. Although Wally wanted to change, he felt that he had "lost control" of his drinking problem. The parents were quite negative about Wally's ability to change. There were no identifiable exceptions and the parents could not describe what a miracle picture would look like. When I asked, "How come things are not worse?," the parents responded with more pessimism. I externalized Wally's "alcoholism problem" into "Alcohol." I explored with the family what a good external symbol would be for alcohol. Wally came up with the idea of using a "beer can" to symbolize Alcohol. While asking externalizing questions, I asked each family member to describe his or her relationship to the imaginary beer can sitting on my end table and what he or she would like to say to it. As a homework assignment, I asked the family to secure an empty beer can and set aside 20 minutes a night to talk as a group to Alcohol and discuss its influence on their lives and relationships. I also requested that they bring Alcohol in with them to the next session. The family came back the following week reporting that there was "less arguing" and Wally had remained alcohol-free. The father shared with me that Wally was "not really the problem," but rather was a "victim of a family disease through the generations." I inquired as to the nature of their discussions about Alcohol and what they had said to it over the past week. The mother had told Alcohol that she would prevent it from "ruining Wally's life." Wally kicked Alcohol across the room after telling it that he would not let it make him "fail in school." I ended up seeing the family four more times over a 6-month period. In our last session together, the family brought in the badly dented beer can, "Alcohol," and great news—Wally had remained alcohol-free for 5 months! The family came up with their own ritual for ending therapy. Each family member took turns stepping on Alcohol and crushing it. After Alcohol was completely flattened out on my office floor, Wally had the honor of dropping it in my garbage can.

I gave all family members high fives for their tremendous victory over "Alcohol."

LETTERS

I like to use letters in therapy as a way to engage important family members and to impact changes in larger systems in which the presenting problem is occurring, particularly in the school context. When I have a case in which the adolescent is having conflict with a particular teacher, I have my identified client's parents prepare a letter for this teacher. The following case is an example of one of my client's letters to a teacher.

Case Example: Ron

Ron had been referred to me for being disruptive in class and getting poor grades. He had a highly conflictive relationship with his English teacher. Ron's mother and I constructed the following letter to his English teacher that Ron was to hand-deliver.

> *Dear Miss Brown:*
>
> *I greatly appreciate your patience and concern with Ron. He can be really difficult to live with at times. I want to see him turn things around in your classroom too. So I gave him an assignment for the day in your class. I have asked him to notice what things you do in the class that he likes and to write those things down and tell me about them tonight. Thank you for everything.*
>
> *Sincerely,*
>
> *Barbara Black*

According to Barbara, Ron came home from school reporting "five" things that he liked about Miss Brown. In fact, the biggest exception was Miss Brown's praising him for coming up with the "right answer" in class. This therapeutic strategy had a major impact on Ron's relationship with Miss Brown. They had developed mutual respect for one another. Ron's disruptive behavior in the classroom stopped and he ended up getting a "B" grade from Miss Brown.

ORDEALS

Erickson developed this type of therapeutic strategy to make it so uncomfortable for the identified client to have the problem that he or she would be glad to give it up (Haley, 1984). Ordeals are particularly useful for altering entrenched symptoms and as a "last resort" therapeutic strategy. I typically utilize this strategy as a form of pattern intervention (O'Hanlon, 1987) with *same* or *worse* clients. The following case of a 12-year-old, recalcitrant, acting-out boy illustrates the use of this therapeutic strategy.

Case Example: Jacob

Jacob had chronically been violating his mother's rules, arguing with her all of the time, abusing alcohol, and cutting classes at school. The mother wanted to change Jacob's breaking curfew problem first. She was at her wits' end with this problem. There were no exceptions nor could she envision future miracles. I asked her in the third session if she were willing to do anything to solve this problem. I told her I had an idea about something we could try if she was ready for it. I instructed the mother to go to a toy store and buy a toy clock. She was to set her alarm clock for 2:00 A.M. and, for the amount of time Jacob came home late after his curfew (10:00 P.M.), she would wake him up and teach him how to tell time. After two more nights of breaking curfew, Jacob quickly discovered the benefits of coming home on time.

STRUCTURED FAMILY FIGHTING TASK

De Shazer (1985) originally developed this therapeutic task for couples that were complaining about a chronic arguing problem. I have found this therapeutic task particularly useful with *same* or *worse* category families in which the chronic arguing problem is identified as the main concern of all family members. Depending on the frequency of the arguments, I will determine how often family fighting times will be scheduled. For example, if the adolescent seems to get into heated arguments with his or her parents four times per week, fighting sessions can be scheduled every other day. The family is to use a kitchen timer and conduct the scheduled fighting sessions outside of the kitchen (more homicides occur in kitchens than anywhere else in the home!). The fighting session begins by flipping a coin to determine who goes first. For 10 minutes one family member can argue with another member. Anything leftover after the 10-minute time period is to be written down on a piece of paper and used in the next scheduled family fighting session. Each family member gets one turn, and no further arguing is allowed outside of the scheduled family fighting times. This therapeutic task is useful for families who report an arguing problem that is out of control, as it serves to disrupt this long-standing pattern of interaction.

SPLITTING THE TEAM

Papp (1983) utilizes what she calls the "Greek chorus" as a team strategy with stuck and entrenched cases. The therapist in the room always takes the pro-change position and sides with the family, while the team members adopt a more pessimistic stability position with the family. Sometimes the team can divide themselves down the middle in terms of change and stability, while the therapist in the room remains neutral.

When working alone, I often bring my pessimistic supervisor into the therapy room in spirit and enlist the family to work with me in proving him wrong. I have found this therapeutic strategy to be particularly effective with chronic adolescent substance-abusing cases (Todd & Selekman, 1991). Some of my difficult adolescent clients have surprised me with their responses to my pessimistic supervisor's predictions about them relapsing in the future. After the first round of proving the pessimistic supervisor wrong, I tell the youth in the next session that the former is "still pessimistic" about him or her "remaining straight" and that "we made a lunch bet over our disagreement about your progress." Adolescents have responded to my pessimistic supervisor's grim predictions with comments like: "I'll save you money on lunch!"; "We will prove him wrong!"; "Where is that guy, he doesn't know nothing!"

PEER REFLECTING TEAM

With some stuck difficult adolescent cases, I explore with the parents and the identified client whether we can enlist the services of the latter's peers who have experienced similar difficulties with their own parents, to serve as consultants to help us out. Once the parents and youth agree to bring in the peers, I ask the parents to call the peers' parents and get their approval to have their son or daughter participate in the therapy. Release of information forms will also be signed to protect client confidentiality.

After the peers have been engaged for the consultation session, they either are positioned behind the family as a group in the therapy room or observe from behind the one-way mirror. Approximately 40 minutes into the hour, we will either turn our chairs around in the therapy room and listen to the peer group's reflections or switch rooms and go behind the one-way mirror to listen to their reflections. The family is in charge of deciding how the reflecting team will be positioned. Following the peer group's 10-minute reflections on our impasse situation, the family and I then reflect on their ideas. In using this peer team strategy, families and I have found the peers' ideas to be highly pragmatic and very creative. The case example below demonstrates the utility of this team strategy.

Case Example: Polly

Polly had been referred to me by her school counselor for "cutting classes," "being truant" from school, and for "conflicts with her teachers." The parents had decided to ground Polly for "two months" as punishment for her school problems. My first two sessions with Polly and her parents were stormy. An intense blame–counterblame pattern of interaction occurred between the threesome. I was without a team on this case and could have greatly benefitted from having one, particularly because I was feeling stuck. In each session, I broke up the family and met separately with the parents and Polly to help disrupt this vicious pattern of interaction. There were no exceptions identified and the family could not envision possible future miracles ever occurring. Neither the parents nor Polly would budge from rigidly maintaining their polarized positions about how things should be. I was unable to negotiate any realistic or solvable treatment goals with the family. While meeting alone with Polly in the second session, I shared with her that I was feeling stuck and wondered if she had any girlfriends who had once had similar difficulties with their parents that we might want to invite to our next session. Polly became quite excited about the prospect of having her friends help us out with her parents. The parents were also receptive to the idea of doing something different and having Polly's friends come to our next family session to help us "brainstorm some new ideas."

In the third session, the atmosphere was lighter in the room and we all waited to hear the peer group's wisdom about what we needed to do differently. Two of Polly's closest friends came to our session. One peer used the metaphor of a "tug-of-war" match to describe what appeared to be going on between Polly and her parents. She also shared that the same "tug-of-war" situation had occurred with her and her parents. Her parent's solution had been to "let go of the rope" and make her fall on her "butt." At that point, she had begun improving her behavior because "putting up a fight was not working." Another peer shared that when her parents had become "less rigid" with the consequences and were willing to make compromises, her behavior had turned around.

When asked to reflect on the peers' reflections, the parents and Polly found hearing their stories informative. Polly's parents began to spontaneously discuss with Polly whether she felt they were being too extreme with the "two-month grounding" situation. This was a different kind of interaction than the former blame–counterblame variety. The end result of this productive family discussion was a quid pro quo contract that I helped negotiate between Polly and her parents. Polly's original grounding period would be reduced to "two weeks," providing Polly would attend her classes and not "mouth off" to her teachers. The peer reflecting team helped us move from a stuck position in treatment and opened up space for new possibilities. Future therapy sessions involved amplifying changes, consolidating gains, and collaborating with school personnel.

TERMINATION IN SOLUTION-ORIENTED BRIEF FAMILY THERAPY

To my mind, when clients can make distinctions between their old problem-saturated beliefs and behavior and their new worldview and exception patterns of interaction, change has clearly occurred. Consolidating questions are effective tools for eliciting family members' "news of a difference." Some helpful consolidating questions to ask in a final session with a family are as follows: "What would you have to do go backwards?"; "What will you have to do to prevent a major backslide?"; "What will you have to continue to do to keep these changes happening?" I also use my trusty imaginary crystal ball (de Shazer, 1985) and my videotape metaphor (O'Hanlon & Weiner-Davis, 1989) to have clients share with me a detailed picture of what future changes they envision themselves making. To conclude this section, I will address the controversial "flight into health" issue in brief therapy below and discuss how I like to celebrate families' therapeutic changes.

FLIGHT INTO HEALTH OR SATISFIED ENOUGH?

When working briefly with families, it is not uncommon after rapid changes occur early in treatment, or while on a longer time interval vacation from therapy, that clients drop out of treatment (Weiner-Davis et al., 1987). Is this flight into health? I do not think so. Clients are quick to tell us if they are experiencing difficulties while they are on a vacation from therapy. Parents do not hesitate to make an emergency appointment when things begin to go backwards or when a crisis occurs. When sending families on vacations from therapy, I am conveying to them my confidence in their ability to cope and function well without me. Similar to my belief that clients should take the lead in determining what the goals of therapy should be, I believe that clients should be in charge of deciding when they would like to stop coming for therapy. As a Solution-Oriented therapist, I do not believe my job is to cure people, but instead, to help clients have more satisfactory life situations. If clients call to cancel future scheduled appointments because they feel things are better for the time being, I always let them know that I have an open door policy and if they need to schedule a future tune-up session, they may feel free to call me.

CELEBRATING THERAPY CHANGES WITH FAMILIES

Whenever possible, I like to make final therapy sessions memorable events. Different cultures worldwide celebrate rites of passage throughout the life cycle with ceremonies and the exchanging of gifts. I like to celebrate a family's rite of passage of moving from a problem-saturated context to a context of change. This end of therapy celebration ritual helps further empower families to take pride and joy in conquering their oppressive problems. I have even thrown parties in probation officers' offices to celebrate my clients getting off of probation. Having been influenced by the innovative work of White and Epston (1990) and Durrant and Coles (1991), I will give family members certificates, pins, trophies, ribbons, and cakes to celebrate their victories over their oppressive problems. The case example below illustrates how I like to celebrate clients' changes at the end of therapy.

Case Example: Bonnie

Bonnie, 16 years old, had been dragged into therapy by her parents for her chronic running away, heavy poly-substance-abuse problems, and gang involvement. After eight sessions of therapy over 6 months time, Bonnie had stopped running away and abusing chemicals. Because the family had had sixteen past therapy experiences, the team and I were quite concerned that the family would spend the rest of their lives in therapy. In order to help break this pattern of family involvement with mental health professionals and further empower the family, I had Bonnie and her mother write their own discharge summary from our therapy experience. In their discharge summary, they were instructed to list all of the changes they had made. They were also asked to mail copies of their discharge summary to all their former therapists. The family generated a list of six major changes they wanted former therapists to read about in their discharge summary, as follows: (1) "We have made it, in spite of all of your diagnoses!"; (2) "You can reason with Bonnie better"; (3) "No more knock down, drag out fights"; (4) "Bonnie doesn't run away"; (5) "Bonnie comes home on time a lot"; and (6) "Bonnie seems to have been straight [drug-free]." Surprisingly, the family did not mention how the running away problem had been resolved. To help make this latter change more "newsworthy," I presented the family with an achievement certificate for "Taming the Running Away Monster." Both Bonnie and her mother were touched by the achievement certificate they had received for conquering the Running Away Monster that had been oppressing them for 5 years.

The next case example illustrates how I like to celebrate when adolescents get off probation in therapy sessions. In some cases, celebrating the termination of probation coincides with the conclusion of therapy.

Case Example: Randy

Randy, a 16-year-old delinquent boy, had been placed on probation for bicycle and car radio theft, marijuana abuse, and frequent police involvement. While on probation, Randy had violated a number of his probationary guidelines and ended up serving a month in the juvenile detention center. While in the "juvie" (Randy's language), Randy had gotten into a fight with a rival gang member. He was placed in solitary confinement for 3 days and was evaluated by the court-appointed psychologist. After completing his psychological testing session with Randy, the psychologist had shared with him that he would most likely end up back in the "juvie" 3 weeks after getting out.

In my first family session with Randy and his mother, I learned about the psychologist's grim prediction. I set up a split between Randy, myself, and the pessimistic psychologist. Randy confidently vowed that he would prove the psychologist wrong by successfully terminating his probation 9 months later. I ended up seeing Randy and his mother six times over a 9-month period. In our sixth and final session together, I brought in a cake to celebrate the end of Randy's probation and the end of therapy. Prior to our last session together, Randy had written a beautiful letter that he planned to send to the psychologist in the "juvie." In the letter, Randy pointed out that he "remembered" the psychologist's prediction that he would end up back in the "juvie" 3 weeks after getting out. Randy also made it clear in his letter that the psychologist had underestimated his strengths and his ability to "turn things around" when the going "gets rough." After Randy read his letter, the mother and I gave him a standing ovation and encouraged him to mail the letter to the psychologist. The remainder of the session involved amplifying and consolidating family gains and having cake to celebrate Randy's great achievement.

Another way I celebrate clients' changes at the end of therapy is to induct them into my "All Star Alumni Association." As part of the induction process, they have to agree when called upon to assist me in the future with my stuck adolescent cases. I have found it quite useful to tap into former clients' expertise and utilize them as guest consultants with other families I am working with or in the Solution-Oriented Parenting groups I am conducting.

S E V E N

THE SOLUTION-ORIENTED
PARENTING GROUP

The Solution-Oriented Parenting group (Selekman, 1991b) was originally developed to serve as a secondary prevention treatment that is an alternative to more traditional 12-step/disease model forms of intervention for the parents of adolescent substance abusers. Many of the parents I have in my parenting groups report having already experienced therapeutic failure in the past when their adolescents were involved in 12-step-oriented outpatient, residential, and hospital-based programs. Frequently, these parents disclosed to fellow group members that they felt like their prior therapists had failed to teach them new parenting strategies for better managing their adolescents' challenging behaviors. The Solution-Oriented Parenting group is not only geared to teach parents "hands-on" parenting skills, but it greatly assists them in becoming more keenly aware of their own parental strengths and resources. Parents also learn creative strategies for accentuating their adolescents' strengths and positive behaviors.

In this chapter, I will discuss my rationale for utilizing the Solution-Oriented Parenting group with difficult adolescent populations, provide guidelines for organizing such groups, describe the role of the group leaders, and present a detailed description of the topics covered in each group meeting. Case examples will be provided throughout.

RATIONALE FOR THE GROUP

It is not always possible to engage difficult adolescents for family therapy. Often, these adolescents are not even "window-shoppers" for therapy and will refuse to attend one session with their parents. The Solution-Oriented Parenting group is a practical treatment alternative that simplifies matters for parents and therapists alike. It helps parents avoid needless power struggles with their adolescents about going for therapy. For therapists, the absence of the adolescent at sessions can reduce complexity, simplify observations, and help us feel less overwhelmed by the available information.

Unlike most parenting groups, the Solution-Oriented Parenting group is wellness based and capitalizes on the strengths and resources of parents to co-construct solutions. The main emphasis of the group is on what is working for the parents, rather than on what the parents are doing wrong with their adolescents. For parents that have already experienced multiple treatment failures with their adolescents, their participation in the Solution-Oriented Parenting group can be an empowering experience for them, particularly when they begin to witness the rapid and beneficial results of the group.

The Solution-Oriented Parenting group is cost effective, making it a treatment service that is marketable to HMOs and managed care companies, which can increase agency referrals. Finally, the Solution-Oriented Parenting group can serve as a potential solution for agency administrators grappling with horrendous waiting lists.

MECHANICS OF ORGANIZING THE GROUP

When organizing a Solution-Oriented Parenting group, it is very important to keep the group homogenous in terms of the age ranges of the adolescents and their presenting problems. Parents of adolescents ranging from 12 to 15 years of age should have a separate group from parents with older adolescents. It is not necessary to have both parents of an adolescent participate in the group, only that parent who is most motivated to do something about his or her adolescent's problematic behavior. In terms of group size, I like to limit the group to no more than eight parents. The Solution-Oriented Parenting group is a closed group.

When marketing the group, it is helpful to put together a detailed flyer describing the group and the dates it is offered. The flyer should be sent to prime referral sources. Some of the best referral sources for recruiting potential group members are as follows: Tough Love and Families Anonymous, probation officers, schools, and churches.

ROLE OF THE GROUP LEADERS

Ideally, a male–female cotherapy team should run the group to provide gender balance. The group leaders are responsible for creating a therapeutic climate for change. This is accomplished through the use of rapport building, purposeful systemic interviewing, giving compliments, giving homework assignments, and consolidating parental gains. The leaders can role-play with each other to demonstrate the various ways parents inadvertently maintain the problem and to teach new parenting strategies. Each group session is 1½ hours in length. At the 45-minute point in the session, the leaders and the group participants take a 15-minute break. During the break time, the leaders generate compliments for the group as a whole and two compliments for each participant. Refreshments are provided for the group members.

GROUP SESSIONS

The Solution-Oriented Parenting group meets six times, with longer time intervals between Sessions 2 through 6. The longer time intervals between sessions serve as a vote of confidence that the parents will continue to develop their new parental skills and notice changes in their adolescents' behaviors as a result of their parental efforts. The six session topic areas covered are as follows:

1. Solution-Oriented Parenting: A New Way of Viewing and Doing
2. Going for Small Changes
3. If It Works, Don't Fix It
4. If It Doesn't Work, Do Something Different
5. Keeping Change Happening
6. Celebrating Change

SESSION 1

In the first group meeting, the leaders begin the session by establishing rapport with each group member. This entails having the parents share information about their interests, occupations, strengths, and talents with one another. The leaders need to listen very carefully to the specific parental strengths and talents that can be utilized in the parents' various problem areas. After joining with each group member, the leaders need to explore with the parents the "why now" of their decision to pursue the parenting group at this time. The remainder of the group time is used by the leaders to teach parents seven key Solution-Oriented assumptions, which are as follows:

1. Change is inevitable.
2. Cooperation is inevitable.
3. Parents and adolescents have the strengths and resources to change.
4. Only a small change is necessary.
5. Problems are unsuccessful attempts to resolve difficulties.
6. You don't need to know a great deal about the problem in order to solve it.
7. There are many ways to look at a situation, none more "correct" than others.

For further details about these assumptions, see Chapter 2 of this book. Each one of these assumptions is presented in a concrete fashion. The group leaders can utilize role-plays and illustrations on a blackboard to highlight key points. At the end of the group meeting, the parents are individually given compliments and are instructed to try as an experiment the "formula first session task" (de Shazer, 1985). As part of the experiment, the parents are to write down all of the exceptions they observe happening in their relationships with their adolescents in 1 week's time and bring their lists in to the next session.

SESSION 2

The second group meeting begins with the leaders asking the parents, "So what's better!?" Each parent is given equal floor time to report the exceptions they observed happening in their relationships with their adolescents. One parent once brought in a four-page list of exceptions she had observed in her adolescent's behavior in a week's time. This parent still holds the all-time Solution-Oriented Parenting group house record for noticing the most exceptions in the shortest amount of time.

The leaders respond to each parental exception with

cheerleading responses such as: "Wow!" "How did you do that!?"; "How did you get that to happen!?"; "Is it different for your [son or daughter] to do that!?" Parental exception patterns are further amplified by the leaders through the use of exception-oriented and presuppositional questions (O'Hanlon & Weiner-Davis, 1989) such as: "What will you have to continue to do to get that [the exception] to happen more often?"; "What else will you have to continue to do?"; "If you were to gaze into my imaginary crystal ball two weeks down the road when things have gotten even better between you and your [son or daughter], what further changes would we see in the crystal ball?"; "What else will be different?" Unique account and redescription questions (White, 1988b) can be utilized to highlight changes in parental self-perceptions following the occurrence of meaningful exceptions.

For those parents who cannot identify any exceptions, the leaders utilize the miracle question (de Shazer, 1988). The remainder of the session is utilized by the leaders to negotiate small and realistic treatment goals with the parents. Scaling questions (de Shazer, 1985) are useful tools for assisting parents with goal setting. After being given group and individual compliments, the parents are instructed to do the following over the next 2 weeks: "Notice the various steps you will take towards achieving your goals. Keep track of your kids' responses when you take those important steps. We will discuss the important steps that you all will have taken at the next meeting."

SESSION 3

Two weeks later, the leaders begin the group session by asking, "So what further progress have all of you made?" All parental exceptions and changes are amplified by the leaders through cheerleading responses and presuppositional questions (O'Hanlon & Weiner-Davis, 1989). For those parents feeling stuck and unable to impact changes in their sons' or daughters' behaviors, the leaders ask, "How come things are not worse?"; "What specifically are you or your [husband or wife] doing to prevent things from getting worse?" These coping questions (Berg & Gallagher, 1991) often elicit important parental exceptions that can be amplified and utilized in the solution construction process. The leaders spend the remainder of the group time teaching parents the importance of "doing more of what works." Parents may be asked if they can think of any past attempted solutions that they previously used that worked with their adolescents, which they think might be useful with their adolescents' present problematic behaviors. It is important for parents to know that their past successes can serve as models for present and future successes.

The leaders may role-play one of the parent's relationship situations with his or her adolescent to illustrate both what is working in their interactions with one another and the consequences of discontinuing the exception-oriented interactive steps. As the group meeting concludes, the leaders give compliments to the group and each parent, and remind the parents that "if it works, don't fix it; do more of what works." The parents are given a 3-week vacation from the group as a vote of confidence.

SESSION 4

In the fourth group session, the group members are asked about further progress they have made toward achieving their goals and generating exceptions with their adolescents' behaviors. Unique account and redescription questions can be utilized to highlight further changes in parental self-perceptions (White, 1988b). By the third and fourth meetings, parents have a tendency to spontaneously cheerlead for and compliment one another. After amplifying and consolidating parental gains, the leaders use the remainder of the group time to teach the parents the importance of "doing something different," when their attempted solutions are not working and they are stuck doing "more of the same" (Watzlawick et al., 1974). With those parents in the group that are feeling stuck doing "more of the same" (Watzlawick et al., 1974), the leaders role-play how the parents get stuck with their adolescents, and the other group members are asked to brainstorm together potential solutions, which are then listed on the blackboard. When doing this exercise, I have been amazed by the creative ingenuity of parents. The stuck parents find this exercise to be a very empowering experience for them. At the same time, the exercise opens up space for new possibilities, in that it gives the stuck parents "hands-on" parental peer-utilized strategies that have worked. The following case example illustrates the power in this group exercise.

Case Example: Gladys

Gladys, an African-American single parent, was feeling totally frustrated with her 16-year-old son, Winston. She had "tried everything" she could possibly think of to get him to "stop stealing money" from her, but nothing had worked. Her past parental attempted solutions had consisted of the following: "yelling," "grounding," "taking away his stereo," trying to get him to family counseling, and "buying him things." When my colleague and I had the group brainstorm some new ideas for Gladys, they came up with the following suggestions: come up with some "house projects" for which Winston could "earn money"; "press charges with the police"; "go on strike as a parent"—that is, "stop cooking" for him and "washing his clothes"; "buy paper money" at a toy store and "hide it" throughout "the house" where she typically kept her money; and "act off-the-wall around Winston" rather than "yell at him." Out of all of the group members ideas, Gladys decided to try making a "game out of the paper money" suggestion, by telling Winston he needed to "find hidden money in the house." In the subsequent group meetings, Gladys had no further complaints about Winston's stealing behavior. The biggest surprise was hearing from Gladys that she could tell that Winston had located where the paper money had been hidden, but that he did not take any of it. It was the group's feeling that Gladys had outwitted Winston and was back in charge as the parent.

Before receiving the homework assignment, the group and each parent are given compliments. Those parents feeling stuck are instructed to do the "do something different task" (de Shazer, 1985). The parents that have already achieved their goals, or are well on their way to goal attainment, are asked to "keep track of what's working and do more of it." As a vote of confidence, the leaders end the group session by giving the parents a 4-week vacation from the group.

SESSION 5

The majority of the fifth group session consists of the leaders amplifying and consolidating the parents' changes. The leaders highlight key parental differences and have each parent make distinctions between his or her old patterns of behavior and the new interactions around his or her adolescent. Parents are asked the following questions by the leaders: "What would you have to do to go backwards?"; "What would you have to do to prevent a major parental backslide?"; "What will you have to continue to do to keep your changes happening?"; "Let's say I were a fly on your living room wall watching you and your [son or daughter] six months down the road, what further changes will I notice with you as a parent and in your relationship with your [son or daughter]?"; "If we were to invite you to our next parents' group as expert consultants, what helpful advice or pointers would you give to those parents?" These questions help elicit the parents' "news of a difference" (Bateson, 1972) and consolidate important parental gains. For those parents who were assigned the do something different task (de Shazer, 1985), the leaders cheerlead and amplify their creative new parenting strategies.

In one of my Solution-Oriented Parenting groups for Latino parents with court-involved adolescents, two of the fathers came up with some very creative and effective parental strategies that were different than their typical course of action. One of the fathers decided to move his son's bed into the middle of the living room in response to his chronically breaking curfew. The boy was so shocked to find his bed in the living room that he started to come home on time in the evenings. The other Latino father posted the parental rules on every door in the house so his son could not escape from what was expected of him. The parents in this case had given up their problem-maintaining behaviors of yelling and lecturing. They discovered that the written word was more powerful than the spoken word.

Frequently, other parents in the group spontaneously applaud the previously stuck parents for taking important steps toward solution with their difficult adolescents. Sometimes, the stuck parents have successfully implemented some of the creative strategies generated by their parental peers in the fourth group session. Finally, as the leaders conclude the meeting they compliment the group and each parent, prescribe "more of what's working" for homework, and extend a warm invitation to the parents to come to their own celebration party in honor of their becoming "Solution-Oriented Parents!" For parents that are still stuck and not reporting exceptions, the group leaders prescribe the "pretend the miracle happened" task (de Shazer, 1991). While pretending their miracle behaviors, the parents are instructed to notice how their adolescents respond differently to them.

SESSION 6

In the final group session, the leaders put together a festive party to celebrate the parents moving from a problem-saturated context to a context of change with their adolescents. The celebration party serves as an important context marker for highlighting and consolidating parental changes in the group. For those parents that experimented with the "pretend the miracle happened" task (de Shazer, 1991), positive parental gains are amplified and consolidated as part of the celebration process. The leaders provide a table of snack foods, refreshments, and a large sheet cake for the parents. Written on the cake is: "Congratulations! Solution-Oriented Parents!" As part of the celebration festivities, each parent receives a Solution-Oriented Parent achievement certificate and is asked to give a speech reflecting on his or her growth as a parent. Once handed their certificates, the parents are officially inducted into the leaders' Solution-Oriented Parents' Alumni Association. When called upon for duty by the leaders, alumni serve as helpful consultants for future parents' groups and may be utilized in the leaders' family therapy sessions to help stuck parents. The leaders conclude the celebration festivities by providing their own reflections on each parent's achievements in the group.

With a small percentage of the group participants, their adolescents may still be having behavioral difficulties at the conclusion of the group. When approached by the parents, the leaders will offer individual family therapy. I do not view these parents as group failures, but as special parental cases where more direct work with them and their adolescents is necessary. It has been my experience, however, that just by having participated in the Solution-Oriented Parenting group, these parents tend to be more unified and better prepared for family therapy.

E I G H T

EPILOGUE

PATHWAYS TO CHANGE REVISITED

Throughout this book, I have presented many challenging theoretical ideas and therapeutic strategies that can increase effectiveness when working with difficult adolescents and their families. At this point, I will review and summarize some of the important ideas discussed in this book.

To begin with, a central underlying theme is my strong belief that all adolescents and their families have the strengths and resources to change. In my view this is one of the most important assumptions for therapists to adopt with *all* families who walk through their office doors. Furthermore I believe that the most important therapeutic task to accomplish in the first interview is to get our clients to do more of what they do best, by capitalizing on their strengths and resources to collaboratively co-construct solutions.

Another important idea that I have presented in the book is the necessity for brief therapists to collaborate actively with the key resource people in the adolescent client's social ecology. Family–multiple helper meetings can empower the family and help them resolve their difficulties rapidly. Several case examples presented earlier demonstrated the therapeutic effectiveness of actively involving the peers of the adolescent client, school personnel, probation officers, and agency therapists in the treatment process. I have also stressed that it is important for therapists to view involved helpers from larger systems as therapeutic allies, not as "the enemy" or "Drs. Homeostats"

(Bergman, 1985). These important resource people deserve the same respect that we give our clients.

When working with difficult adolescent cases, brief therapists need to be able to serve as intergenerational negotiators working both sides of the fence. Far too many therapists invest most of their therapeutic energy in empowering the parents without attending to the goals and expectations of the adolescents in their cases, which can lead to the latter dropping out of therapy. Most adolescent clients, when asked, will tell therapists how to cooperate with them and what they want to change about themselves and their families. With those adolescent clients who have had past therapy experiences, it is helpful to tap into their expertise about what they liked and disliked about former therapists, so as to avoid making the same mistakes.

A final idea I wish to touch on is my belief that therapy is a creative art form. The therapeutic context is a stage for improvisation, creativity, and playfulness on the part of the therapist. For any one family theme, there is a multiplicity of ways the brief therapist can improvise. Similar to a skillful jazz saxophonist, I like to begin an interview playing the family's central theme, gradually blowing notes that are outside the family's musical score through the use of humor and storytelling and eventually to cocreate with the family a new musical score that combines elements from the old and new scores. At times, I will really push the limits of my playing to generate laughter among family members, which helps them experience themselves and their relationships differently, thus opening up space for new possibilities.

CONCLUSION

In this book I have presented an integrative Solution-Oriented Brief Therapy approach that offers clinicians multiple pathways for providing effective treatment with difficult adolescents and their families. The treatment approach is ecosystemic and goal-oriented, and views families through a wellness lens. Therapy is collaborative and capitalizes on the strengths and resources of adolescents, their families, and involved helpers from larger systems to rapidly co-construct solutions.

Working in the trenches with difficult adolescents and their families can be a challenge for the most seasoned of therapists. It is my hope that the ideas discussed in this book will help keep therapists alive, will stimulate therapeutic creativity, and will provide therapists with a renewed sense of optimism in their day-to-day clinical work with difficult adolescent cases.

REFERENCES

Alexander, J. F., Barton, C., Schiavo, R. S., & Parsons, B. V. (1976). Systems-behavioral intervention with families of delinquents: Therapist characteristics, family behavior, and outcome. *Journal of Consulting and Clinical Psychology, 44,* 656–664.

Andersen, T. (1987). The reflecting team: Dialogue and meta-dialogue in clinical work. *Family Process, 26*(4), 415–428.

Andersen, T. (1991). *The reflecting team: Dialogue and dialogues about the dialogues.* New York: W. W. Norton.

Anderson, H., & Goolishian, H. (1988a). *Changing thoughts on self, agency, questions, narrative and therapy.* Unpublished manuscript.

Anderson, H., & Goolishian, H. (1988b). Human systems as linguistic systems: Evolving ideas about the implications for theory and practice. *Family Process, 27,* 371–393.

Anderson, H., & Goolishian, H. (1991a). Thinking about multiagency work with substance abusers and their families: A language systems approach. *Journal of Strategic and Systemic Therapies, 10*(1), 20–36.

Anderson, H., & Goolishian, H. (1991b, October). *"Not-knowing": A critical element of a collaborative language systems therapy approach.* Plenary address presented at the 1991 Annual American Association for Marriage and Family Therapy Conference, Dallas, TX.

Anderson, H., Goolishian, H., Pulliam, G., & Winderman, L. (1986). The Galveston Family Institute: Some personal and historical perspectives. In D. Efron (Ed.), *Journeys: Expansion of the strategic–systemic therapies* (pp. 97–125.). New York: Brunner/ Mazel.

American Psychiatric Association. (1987). *Diagnostic and statistical manual of mental disorders* (3rd ed., rev.). Washington, DC: Author.

Auerswald, E. H. (1968). Interdisciplinary versus ecological approach. *Family Process, 7,* 202–215.

Auerswald, E. H. (1972). Families, change, and the ecological perspective. In A. Ferber, M. Mendelsohn, & A. Napier (Eds.), *The book of family therapy* (pp. 684–706). New York: Science House.

Barton, C., & Alexander, J. F. (1981). Functional family therapy. In A. S. Gurman & D. P. Kniskern (Eds.), *Handbook of family therapy* (pp. 403–443). New York: Brunner/Mazel.

Bateson, G. (1972). *Steps to an ecology of mind.* New York: Ballantine Books.

Bateson, G. (1980). *Mind and nature: A necessary unity.* New York: Ballantine Books.

Beavers, W. R., & Hampson, B. (1990). *Successful families.* New York: W. W. Norton.

Bennis, W. (1976). *The unconscious conspiracy: Why leaders can't lead.* New York: AMACOM.

Berg, I. K., & Gallagher, D. (1991). Solution-focused brief therapy with adolescent substance abusers. In T. C. Todd & M. D. Selekman (Eds.), *Family therapy approaches with adolescent substance abusers* (pp. 93–111). Needham Heights, MA: Allyn & Bacon.

Bergman, J. S. (1985). *Fishing for barracuda: Pragmatics of brief systemic therapy.* New York: W. W. Norton.

Black, E. I. (1988). *Families and larger systems.* New York: Guilford Press.

Bodin, A. (1981). The interactional view: Family therapy appproaches of the Mental Research Institute. In A. S. Gurman & D. P. Kniskern (Eds.), *Handbook of family therapy* (pp. 267–309). New York: Brunner/Mazel.

Bogdan, J. (1984). Family organization as an ecology of ideas. *Family Process, 23,* 375–388.

Boscolo, L., Cecchin, G., Hoffman, L., & Penn, P. (1987). *Milan systemic family therapy: Conversations in therapy and practice.* New York: Basic Books.

Breunlin, D. C., Schwartz, R. C., & MacKune-Karrer, B. (1992). *Metaframeworks: Transcending the models of family therapy.* San Francisco: Jossey-Bass.

Coltrane, J. (1967, September). [Untitled article]. *Jazz & Pop,* p. 26.

Coppersmith, E. I. (1985). Families and multiple helpers: A systemic perspective. In D. Campbell & R. Draper (Eds.), *Applications of systemic family therapy: A Milan approach.* London: Grune & Stratton.

DeFrain, J., & Stinnett, N. (1992). Building on the inherent strengths of families: A positive approach for family psychologists and counselors. *Topics in Family Psychology and Counseling, 1*(1), 15–26.

Deissler, K. G. (1989). Co-menting: Toward a systemic poietology? *Continuing the Conversation, Fall, 18,* 1–10.

Deissler, K. G. (1992). *Systemic studies of cooperation in the context of a mental state hospital.* Unpublished manuscript.

Dembo, R. (1992, June). *Plenary overview of consensus panel on screening and assessment of substance-abusing adolescents.* Consensus panel address for "Treatment of Substance-Abusing Adolescents," Office for Treatment Improvement, Alcohol, Drug Abuse, and Mental Health Administration, Washington, DC.

de Shazer, S. (1982). Some conceptual distinctions are more useful than others. *Family Process, 21,* 71–84.

de Shazer, S. (1984). The death of resistance. *Family Process, 23,* 79–93.

de Shazer, S. (1985). *Keys to solution in brief therapy.* New York: W. W. Norton.

de Shazer, S. (1988). *Clues: Investigating solutions in brief therapy.* New York: W. W. Norton.

de Shazer, S. (1990). *What is it about brief therapy that works.* J. K. Zeig & S. G. Gilligan (Eds.), *Brief therapy: Myths, methods and metaphors* (pp. 90–100). New York: Brunner/Mazel.

de Shazer, S. (1991). *Putting difference to work.* New York: W. W. Norton.

de Shazer, S., Berg, I. K., Lipchik, E., Nunnally, E., Molnar, A., Gingerich, W., & Weiner-Davis, M. (1986). Brief therapy: Focused solution development. *Family Process, 25,* 207–222.

Durrant, M., & Coles, D. (1991). The Michael White approach. In T. C. Todd & M. D. Selekman (Eds.), *Family therapy approaches with adolescent substance abusers* (pp. 135–175). Needham Heights, MA: Allyn & Bacon.

Efran, J., & Lukens, M. (1985). The world according to Humberto Maturana. *Family Therapy Networker, May–June,* 23–28, 72–75.

Erickson, M. H. (1954). Pseudo-orientation in time as a hypnotic procedure. *Journal of Clinical and Experimental Hypnosis, 2,* 161–283.

Erickson, M. H. (1964). The confusion technique in hypnosis. *American Journal of Clinical Hypnosis, 6,* 183–207.

Erickson, M. H., & Rossi, E. (1983). *Healing in hypnosis.* New York: Irvington.

Erickson, M. H., Rossi, E., & Rossi, I. (1976). *Hypnotic realities*. New York: Irvington.

Fisch, R., Weakland, J., & Segal, L. (1982). *The tactics of change*. San Francisco: Jossey-Bass.

von Foerster, H. (1981). *Observing systems*. Seaside, CA: Intersystems.

Friesen, J. D., Grigg, D. N., & Newman, J. A. (1991). *Experiential systemic therapy: An overview*. Unpublished manuscript.

Fuller, J. (1992, March). Lost and found: John Coltrane's lifelong quest for a new direction. *Chicago Tribune*, sec. 13, p. 22.

Gingerich, W., de Shazer, S., & Weiner-Davis, M. (1988). Constructing change: A research view of interviewing. In E. Lipchik (Ed.), *Interviewing* (pp. 21–31). Rockville, MD: Aspen.

Gingerich, W., & de Shazer, S. (1991). The BRIEFER project: Using expert systems as theory construction tools. *Family Process, 30,* 241–249.

von Glasersfeld, E. (1984). An introduction to radical constructivism. In P. Watzlawick (Ed.), *The invented reality* (pp. 17–40). New York: W. W. Norton.

Glassner, B., & Loughlin, J. (1987). *Drugs in adolescent worlds: Burnouts to straights*. New York: St. Martin's Press.

Goolishian, H. (1991, October). *The dis-diseasing of mental health*. Plenary address presented at the Houston–Galveston Institute's Conference II, San Antonio, TX.

Goolishian, H., & Anderson, H. (1981). Including non-blood related persons in family therapy. In A. S. Gurman (Ed.), *Questions and answers in the practice of family therapy* (pp. 75–80). New York: Brunner/Mazel.

Gordon, D., & Meyers-Anderson, M. (1981). *Phoenix: Therapeutic patterns of Milton H. Erickson*. Cupertino, CA: Meta.

Gurin, J. (1990, March). Remaking our lives. *American Health*, pp. 50–52.

Haley, J. (1984). *Ordeal therapy*. San Francisco: Jossey-Bass.

Hammerschlag, C. (1988). *The dancing healers: A doctor's journey of healing with Native Americans*. New York: Harper & Row.

Harrison, P. A., & Hoffman, N. G. (1987). *CATOR 1987 report: Adolescent residential treatment intake and follow-up findings*. St. Paul, MN: Chemical Abuse/Addiction Treatment Outcome Registry.

Hentoff, N. (1958). Liner notes for *Something Else! The music of Ornette Coleman*. Contemporary 7551.

Hoffman, L. (1988). A constructivist position for family therapy. *The Irish Journal of Psychology, 9,* 110–129.

Jones, R. A. (1977). *Self-fulfilling prophecies: Social, psychological and physiological effects of expectancies.* Hillsdale, NJ: Erlbaum.

Katz, S. J., & Liu, A. E. (1991). *The codependency conspiracy.* New York: Warner Books.

Kearney, P., Byrne, N. O., & McCarthy, I. M. (1989). Just metaphors: Marginal illuminations in a colonial retreat. *Family Therapy Case Studies, 4*(1), 17–33.

Keeney, B., & Ross, J. (1983). Cybernetics of brief family therapy. *Journal of Marital and Family Therapy, 9,* 375–382.

Kissen, B., Platz, A., & Su, W. H. (1971). Selective factors in treatment choice and outcome in alcoholism. In N. K. Mello & J. H. Mendelsohn (Eds.), *Recent advances in studies of alcoholism* (pp. 781–802). Washington, DC: U. S. Government Printing Office.

Leake, G. J., & King, A. S. (1977). Effect of counselor expectations on alcoholic recovery. *Alcohol, Health and Resource World, 11*(3), 16–22.

Lipchik, E. (1988, Winter). Interviewing with a constructive ear. *Dulwich Centre Newsletter,* 3–7. (Available from Dulwich Centre Publications, Hutt Street, P.O. Box 7192, Adelaide, South Australia 5000).

Lipchik, E., & de Shazer, S. (1986). The purposeful interview. *Journal of Strategic and Systemic Therapies, 5*(1), 88–99.

Lussardi, D. J., & Miller, D. (1991). A reflecting team approach to adolescent substance abuse. In T. C. Todd & M. D. Selekman (Eds.), *Family therapy approaches with adolescent substance abusers* (pp. 227–240). Needham Heights, MA: Allyn & Bacon.

Madanes, C. (1984). *Behind the one-way mirror.* San Francisco: Jossey-Bass.

Maruyama, M. (1974). The second cybernetics: Deviation-amplifying mutual causative processes. *American Scientist, 51,* 164–179.

Maturana, H., & Varela, F. (1988). *The tree of knowledge: The biological roots to human understanding.* Boston: New Science Library.

McCarthy, I. M., & Byrne, N. O. (1988). Mis-taken love: Conversations on the problem of incest in an Irish context. *Family Process, 27,* 181–199.

Miller, W. R. (1985). Motivation for treatment: A review with special emphasis on alcoholism. *Psychological Bulletin, 98,* 84–107.

Miller, W. R., & Sovereign, R. G. (1989). The checkup: A model for early intervention in addictive behaviors. In T. Loberg, W. R. Miller, P. E. Nathan, & G. A. Marlott (Eds.), *Addictive behaviors: Prevention and early intervention* (pp. 219–231). Amsterdam: Swets & Zietlinger.

Minuchin, S. (1974). *Families and family therapy.* Cambridge, MA: Harvard University Press.

Mitchell, S. (1988). *Tao Te Ching: A new English version.* New York: HarperCollins.

Molnar, A., & de Shazer, S. (1987). Solution-focused therapy: Toward the identification of therapeutic tasks. *Journal of Marital and Family Therapy, 13*(4), 349–358.

Newfield, N. A., Kuehl, B. P., Joanning, H. P., & Quinn, W. H. (1991). We can tell you about "psychos" and "shrinks": An ethnography of the family therapy of adolescent drug abuse. In T. C. Todd & M. D. Selekman (Eds.), *Family therapy approaches with adolescent substance abusers* (pp. 277–310). Needham Heights, MA: Allyn & Bacon.

O'Hanlon, W. H. (1987). *Taproots: Underlying principles of Milton H. Erickson's therapy and hypnosis.* New York: W. W. Norton.

O'Hanlon, W. H., & Weiner-Davis, M. (1989). *In search of solutions: A new direction in psychotherapy.* New York: W. W. Norton.

Orford, J., & Hawker, A. (1974). An investigation of an alcoholism rehabilitation halfway house: II. The complex question of client motivation. *British Journal of Addiction, 69,* 315–323.

Palazzoli, M. S. (1980). Why a long interval between sessions? The therapeutic control of the family–therapist suprasystem. In M. Andolfi & I. Zwerling (Eds.), *Dimensions of family therapy* (pp. 161–171). New York: Guilford Press.

Palazzoli, M. S., Boscolo, L., Cecchin, G., & Prata, G. (1980). Hypothesizing—circularity—neutrality: Three guidelines for the conductor of the session. *Family Process, 19*(1), 3–13.

Papp, P. (1983). *The process of change.* New York: Guilford Press.

Parker, M. W., Winstead, D. K., & Willi, F. J. (1979). Patient autonomy in alcohol rehabilitation: Literature review. *International Journal of the Addictions, 14,* 1015–1022.

Parsons, B. V., & Alexander, J. F. (1973). Short-term family intervention: A therapy outcome study. *Journal of Consulting and Clinical Psychology, 41,* 195–201.

Patterson, G. R., & Forgatch, M. I. (1985). Therapist behavior as a determinant for client noncompliance: A paradox for the behavior modifier. *Journal of Consulting and Clinical Psychology,* *53,* 846–851.

Peele, S. (1989). *Diseasing of America: Addiction treatment out of control.* Lexington, MA: Lexington Books.

Penn, P. (1985). Feed forward: Future questions, future maps. *Family Process, 24*(3), 299–310.

Peters, T. J., & Waterman, R. H. (1982). *In search of excellence: Lessons from America's best-run companies.* New York: Warner Books.

Rosen, S. (1982). *My voice will go with you: The teaching tales of Milton H. Erickson.* New York: W. W. Norton.

Sanchez-Craig, M., & Lei, H. (1986). Disadvantages of imposing the goal of abstinence on problem drinkers: An empirical study. *British Journal of Addiction, 81,* 505–512.

Selekman, M. D. (1989a). Taming chemical monsters: Cybernetic–systemic therapy with adolescent substance abusers. *Journal of Strategic and Systemic Therapies, 8*(3), 5–10.

Selekman, M. D. (1989b). Engaging adolescent substance abusers in family therapy. *Family Therapy Case Studies, 4*(1), 67–74.

Selekman, M. D. (1991a). "With a little help from my friends": The use of peers in the family therapy of adolescent substances abusers. *Family Dynamics of Addiction Quarterly, 1*(1), 69–77.

Selekman, M. D. (1991b). The solution-oriented parenting group: A treatment alternative that works. *Journal of Strategic and Systemic Therapies, 10*(1), 36–49.

Selekman, M. D., & Todd, T. C. (1991). Crucial issues in the treatment of adolescent substance abusers and their families. In T. C. Todd & M. D. Selekman (Eds.), *Family therapy approaches with adolescent substance abusers* (pp. 1–20). Needham Heights, MA: Allyn & Bacon.

Sherman, S. J., Skov, R. B., Hervitz, E. F., & Stock, C. B. (1981). The effects of explaining hypothetical future events: From possibility to probability to actuality and beyond. *Journal of Experimental Social Psychology, 17,* 142–157.

Sidran, B. (1971). *Black talk.* New York: DeCapo Press.

Snyder, M., & White, P. (1982). Moods and memories: Elation, depression, and the remembering of the events of one's life. *Journal of Personality, 50*(2), 149–167.

Spanos, N. P., & Radtke, H. L. (1981). Hypnotic visual hallucinations as imaginings: A cognitive–social psychological perspective. *Imagination, Cognition and Personality, 1*(2), 147–170.

Spanos, N. P. (1990). Imagery, hypnosis and hypnotizability. In R. G. Kunzendorf (Ed.), *Mental imagery*. New York: Plenum Press.

Szapocznik, J., Kurtines, W. M., Foote, F. H., Perez-Vidal, A., & Hervis, O. (1983). Conjoint versus one-person family therapy: Some evidence for the effectiveness of conducting family therapy through one person with drug-abusing adolescents. *Journal of Consulting and Clinical Psychology, 51*(6), 889–899.

Szapocznik, J., Kurtines, W. M., Foote, F. H., Perez-Vidal, A., & Hervis, O. (1986). Conjoint versus one-person family therapy: Further evidence for the effectiveness of conducting family therapy through one person with drug-abusing adolescents. *Journal of Consulting and Clinical Psychology, 54*(3), 395–397.

Thorton, C. C., Gottheil, E., Gellens, H. K., & Alterman, A. I. (1977). Voluntary versus involuntary abstinence in the treatment of alcoholics. *Journal of Studies on Alcohol, 38*, 1740–1748.

Todd, T. C., & Selekman, M. D. (1991). Beyond structural–strategic family therapy: Integrating other brief systemic therapies. In T. C. Todd & M. D. Selekman (Eds.), *Family therapy approaches with adolescent substance abusers* (pp. 241-271). Needham Heights, MA: Allyn & Bacon.

Tomm, K. (1987) Interventive interviewing: Part II. Reflexive questioning as a means to enable self-healing. *Family Process, 26*, 167–183.

Tomm, K. (1990). A critique of the DSM. Dulwich Centre Newsletter, 3, 5–9. (Available from Dulwich Centre Publications, Hutt Street, P. O. Box 7192, Adelaide, South Australia 5000).

Tomm, K., & White, M. (1987, October) *Externalizing problems and internalizing directional choices*. Paper presented at the Annual American Association for Marriage and Family Therapy Conference, Chicago, IL.

Wall, S., & Arden, H. (1990). *Wisdomkeepers: Meetings with Native American spiritual elders*. Hillsboro, OR: Beyond Words.

Watzlawick, P., Weakland, J., & Fisch, R. (1967). *Pragmatics of human communication*. New York: W. W. Norton.

Watzlawick, P., Weakland, J., & Fisch, R. (1974). *Change: Principles of problem formation and problem resolution*. New York: W. W. Norton.

Weakland, J. H., & Jordan, L. (1990). Working briefly with reluctant clients: Child protective services as an example. *Family Therapy Case Studies, 5*(2), 51–68.

Weiner-Davis, M. (1992). *Divorce busting.* New York: Simon & Schuster.

Weiner-Davis, M., de Shazer, S., & Gingerich, W. (1987). Building on pretreatment change to construct the therapeutic solution: An exploratory study. *Journal of Marital and Family Therapy, 13,*(4), 359–363.

White, M. (1984). Pseudo-encopresis: From avalanche to victory, from vicious to virtuous cycles. *Family Systems Medicine, 2*(2), 150–160.

White, M. (1985). Fear-busting and monster taming: An approach to the fears of young children. *Dulwich Centre Review,* 29–33. (Available from Dulwich Centre Publications, Hutt Street, P.O. Box 7192, Adelaide, South Australia 5000).

White, M. (1986). Negative explanation, restraint and double description: A template for family therapy. *Family Process, 25*(2), 169–184.

White, M. (1987). Family therapy and schizophrenia: Addressing the in-the-corner lifestyle. *Dulwich Centre Newsletter,* 14–21. (Available from Dulwich Centre Publications, Hutt Street, P.O. Box 7192, Adelaide, South Australia 5000).

White, M. (1988a). Anorexia nervosa: A cybernetic perspective. In J. E. Harkaway (Ed.), *Eating disorders* (pp. 117–129). Rockville, MD: Aspen.

White, M. (1988b, Winter). The process of questioning: A therapy of literary merit? *Dulwich Centre Newsletter,* 8–14. (Available from Dulwich Centre Publications, Hutt Street, P.O. Box 7192, Adelaide, South Australia 5000).

White, M., & Epston, D. (1990). *Narrative means to therapeutic ends.* New York: W. W. Norton.

Whitfield, S. (1992). *Magritte.* London: South Bank Centre.

Williams, M. (1939). *Jazz panorama.* New York: Harcourt.

Wolin, S. (1991, October). *The challenge model: How children rise above adversity.* Plenary address presented at the 1991 Annual American Association for Marriage and Family Therapy Conference, Dallas, TX.

INDEX